UPHILL CLIMB

by DONNA MARTONFI

Foreword

by FRED FULFORD

Bog VAS BLAGOSLOVI

Donna Martonfi — West

(ČORAK)

519-442-5771

Copyright Donna Martonfi
110 East River Road
Paris, Ontario N3L 3E1

www.donnamartonfi.com

Revised Edition 2011

Edited by: Arlie Norman

All rights reserved. This publication may not be reproduced, stored in a retrieval system, or transmitted in whole or in part, in any form or by any means, electronic, mechanical, photocopying, recording or otherwise, without the prior written permission of the Author.

Table of Contents

Dedications

Foreword

Chapter One
DIANA -- A BEAUTIFUL TRAGEDY

Chapter Two
A LITTLE BIT O' HAPPINESS

Chapter Three
MIRACLE ... PROBABLY A FIGMENT OF YOUR IMAGINATION

Chapter Four
HAPPY ... WOULDN'T YOU BE?

Chapter Five
ANOTHER MIRACLE? -- SOUNDS MORE LIKE A MISTAKE

Chapter Six
A VERY LONG HORROR STORY

Chapter Seven
CLOSE ENCOUNTERS WITH THE LIVING GOD

Chapter Eight
NOW YOU'RE GONNA SEE MIRACLES!

Chapter Nine
THINGS GO BETTER WITH GOD

Chapter Ten
SO UNBELIEVABLE -- IT'S BELIEVABLE

Chapter Eleven
BE PATIENT -- GOD'S NOT FINISHED WITH ME YET

Chapter Twelve
GO TELL IT ON THE MOUNTAIN

Dedications

TO THE LORD JESUS CHRIST

--All the glory and honor and power go to You, Lord

TO MY MOTHER-IN-LAW

--I love you because Jesus loved you first and I've had a glimpse of His love.

TO MY MOTHER

--I do love you, really I do. God chose you to be my mother and I thank Him for the relationship now growing between us.

TO BOTH MOTHERS

Keep these words close to your heart as you read through section one. Treasure them. Cry when I cried -- laugh where I do. This story has a happy ending. PRAISE GOD!

Foreword

The mosaic of modern life is studded with superstars. These "beautiful people" glitter with media attention and the adulation and adoration of the masses. The dazzle of their glamour tends to blind many, I think, to the truth that ordinary people can have rich and exciting lives.

It is seven years since the Lord led Donna into our church and our lives. The wholehearted way that she opened her life to God´s grace has been an inspiration, not only to me, but to our whole church family. If you are like me, you will laugh and cry as you read her story.

Donna is still with us. She is still in love with Jesus. She is still growing. Her life gives eloquent testimony to the fact that one does not have to be a superstar to be chosen and used by God in a significant way. God seems to take delight in using and blessing ordinary people.

Donna is learning that life does not have to be spectacular to be very rich and full. God has ways of making normal, even dismal days very wonderful. There is room in life for the spectacular, and Donna will always be partial to God´s miracles. However, she has learned that the meat of life is living in the ordinary times, with the grace and love of God flowing through her in ordinary ways; content because to live is Christ, nothing more and nothing less.

Jesus is wonderful. Let Donna tell you for herself.

Fred Fulford

Pastor, Mississauga Gospel Temple

Chapter One

DIANA -- A BEAUTIFUL TRAGEDY

Looking for our first home while being nine months pregnant had taken a lot out of me. I asked the real estate agent to leave as soon as we had signed the offer. I was exhausted. This pregnancy, my first, was easier than I thought it would be, until tonight. I must have overdone the house hopping. I was glad it was over. If I didn't ache so much, I would have started packing that night. It wasn't even midnight yet.

Same Night: Just After Midnight -- December 7th 1967

"Honey, how would you like to go for a ride?"

"Go to Sleep," he muttered.

"I'm not kidding. Wake up. Tonight's the night!"

"Donna, are you sure? You're probably mistaken. Where are my socks?"

Somehow, I had always pictured this moment a little differently. I was the one who was usually difficult to wake! I stood there laughing: He had his foot propped on my stomach, and he was hoping I'd go away and come back in the morning.

During the next thirteen hours, I lay planning all the things we were going to do with our new son. The life he would have, the kind of life that Darko and I had been deprived of. We had missed out on so much. Our childhoods were lonely; sad and full of fear -- nothing we would want to reminisce over. But our son's would be filled with love and warmth, beauty and security. He would not need to fear anything, ever. He would grow in bliss each and every day of his life. In a few hours our dream would come true.

Darko and I had looked forward to this moment from the time we met four and a half years ago. He was nineteen and I was a whole grownup, full-fledged, ready to tackle the world, "fifteen". Having waited first to graduate from high school to get married, then till we saved a downpayment for a home (and a red sports car he so desperately wanted), the moment was finally here.

Labor wasn't nearly as bad as I thought it would be. Just keep plugging cigarettes in my mouth, and I'd be the most cooperative, undemanding patient a nurse could ever hope for. Labor was degrading, maybe humiliating, but not half bad. In thirteen hours I lost all the modesty I had ever possessed. Who are all these people? It seemed like everyone in the hospital had seen the baby's head, except me.

"One more hard push, Donna, that's a girl, here it comes. Good. Good." coaxed Dr. Moore.

"Oh, he's crying, let me see him!" My motherly arms ached to hold him.

Silence.

"It's a girl, Donna."

"A g-i-r-l? I wanted a boy so-o-o bad."

"She has a defect, Donna."

Dr. Moore put the baby on my chest. She had a small round hole, about the size of a quarter on her back. I could see inside her body. A nurse hastily pulled her away. "That's not a defect", my mind screamed. "They'll put a bandage on it. Why all the fuss?"

My mind raced back and forth.

"I'm sorry I didn't want a girl."

It wasn't because I didn't like girls. But, I'd be a better mother to a boy. I wouldn't get smothering and mushy. I'd make him do housework and chores and not let him take advantage of my weak points. I'd only spoil a girl rotten, wanting to compensate for my own childhood. Too many responsibilities, at a very young age, with little time for fun and fantasy. I also pictured an awful image of what she would or could look like, being a combination of Darko and myself. We weren't the smallest of people and Darko was a large burly man. She would not be petite, I'm certain and I could just picture her stomping around the house talking in a husky voice like daddy. Would she end up with my huge nose and small ugly teeth? I thought it would be cruel to bring a daughter into this world handicapped with these characteristics.

"I'm sorry, I'M SORRY! I DIDN'T MEAN IT THE WAY IT SOUNDED. I DO WANT A GIRL!" My little girl. "Please, somebody PLEASE say she's all right!"

As my eyes bathed this pretty, dainty, blue eyed, blond baby, I didn't care what she grew up to look like. Looking at her I knew I could be the very best mother any girl could hope for. I just knew they would put a bandage on her back, and my little darling and I would begin life, the way I had always planned.

I was picturing the frilly little dresses, the frilly underpants and going to parks. I foresaw our whole future together in those few minutes.

The delivery room was silent, except for Dr. Moore's soft voice on the phone. "We'll send the mother over too. She'll need a skin graft to enclose her exposed spine."

Looking at this precious little doll, kicking and crying in the incubator, it was hard to believe Dr. Moore said she couldn't live more than a few days without the operation.

I was wheeled to a private room. Don't you usually get a ward bed when you pay for semiprivate coverage? This was a switch. I didn't want to be in a single room, I wouldn't have anyone to talk to.

Darko entered crying so hard he was heaving. He leaned over and just held me as we sobbed. "Why us? Why are our dreams being shattered, Donna?"

Only nineteen and I felt like I was eighty.

I worked hard for what I wanted and was making a salary to prove it. But, I was also used and abused as I always went more than that extra mile. People take advantage when you're a doer; a worker, an achiever.

After I graduated from high school, I was hired to set up the IBM keypunch department for a medium sized company. This was my first job. Within a week I was also doing their "accounts receivable". Second week I was the telex operator because I typed faster than the regular girl. The time saved was money saved, just like on a long-distance call. When the Payroll Clerk quit, they didn't replace him. Instead, I acquired responsibility for the weekly payroll for 140 factory workers. No one wanted to replace the switchboard operator, so I was asked to relieve her for "her" lunch hour, while I ate mine at the reception desk. My problem was; I could speed up. I asked for a raise almost every week, and did receive one; which greatly helped while saving for our large wedding. I knew I couldn't keep up the gruelling pace forever, so after the wedding, when we wouldn't need as much money, I planned to quit. I knew I could manage till then.

The line ups, for various skills and free services, were miles long, and not just at my office. Parents, aunts, uncles, neighbours: "Super Gal Donna. She'll help, she'll do it, she knows how. She's got the youth and the stamina."

Darko and I planned, arranged and paid for our own wedding. It took an entire year of saving and scrimping. Each week, out of my pay check, I would pay for the cooks, the invitations, the band, the hall or the food. It cost thousands of dollars to have 250 guests. My parents wanted me to have the grandest wedding, but Darko and I had to do it on our own. Nobody helped, but everybody offered advice. No one realized it was too big a job -- alone. This was not a talent or natural ability that I was gifted with. It was hard work!

Even though Darko didn't speak a word of English when he arrived in Canada in 1963, he was catching up quickly. He got his electrician's license and was earning top wages, EXCEPT: he signed over the back of his paycheck, as was expected of a good Slavic son, to his mother. He was then given streetcar fare and two cartons of cigarettes for the week. NO allowance whatsoever. Just a box lunch. This left only my paycheck for our 'grand' wedding. Two weeks before our wedding, I didn't have the funds for the bridal party's flowers. We called a family 'Pow Wow'. That's just what it looked like. Our mistake was not having a ´Peace Pipe´. Everyone was sitting around somber, preparing for a cold war. My dad said if we hadn´t saved enough money for the expenses of a wedding, we had no business getting married. His mother said, ´since it was Nick´s daughter getting married, Nick should pay for the flowers´. My mother just cried.

Now looking past Darko as the door opened, I saw my mother crying and sobbing in the hall. "Don´t let my mother in. Please don´t let my mother in this room." Darko went and said something to her. She came in and enveloped me for a moment, then was led out again.

Afternoon, December 9th

Trying to get information about my daughter was called ´pass the buck´. I hadn´t seen ANY doctors. Nurses just insisted they knew nothing and I would have to talk to DOCTORS. ´What doctors?´ No one knew. But happily, since I was still here, in this hospital, that meant no skin graft, which meant -- bandage ONLY. I presumed they had made a big thing of her condition so I´d be prepared for the worst and then be relieved when nothing serious was found.

I was sitting, putting on my face, when Darko came in.

"How do you feel, MUM?"

"Fine, now that you´re here. You know what I´d like to do? -- See some babies. Let´s go to the nursery windows."

"There are no babies on this floor. They´re upstairs." he replied, surprised that I didn´t know.

"What do you mean upstairs? I thought I was ON the ´baby ward´."

"No -- there´s just sick people out there -- no babies."

"Well, let´s go find the babies´ floor."

We roamed the halls and elevators till we found the newborn nursery. With me in my housecoat and gown, no one paid much attention to us. My heart just leaped in my chest when I saw those tiny bundles of joy in pink and blue. I wanted to hold my baby. I just ached for her. Pink and blue everywhere, except -- I noticed a small baby in an incubator laying on its stomach, without a stitch of clothing on. It had a growth on its back about the size of a small child's fist and its feet were pointing curiously toward each other. As a nurse passed, inquisitive being that I am, I asked, "What is that, on the baby's back?"

"Oh she's got spina bifida, she isn't going to live, poor thing." I had heard that word before, -- in the delivery room, -- when Doctor Moore called the other hospital -- "OH MY GOD! -- that's our child!"

My legs turned to jelly and I was on my knees in front of the nursery glass, gasping for air, trying to stay conscious, my head drained of blood.

The young nurse instantly realized what had happened. We were the parents. We didn't know. Two days and she was still here, waiting to die. No skin graft! No operation!

I don't know how I ended up in my bed two floors below. I was hysterical. "Get my doctor. What's happening? What's that on her back? What do you mean, 'GOING TO DIE'?"

Within hours, the word spread among relatives. I was getting phone call after phone call.

"Heard you had a cripple."

"It'll be best if she dies, dear."

"You don't want a crippled child. You should adopt."

"Don't adopt, European husbands could never love someone else's child."

The next soothing comments were my mother-in-law's; "I told you that you shouldn't smoke. See what you did now? God's punishing you for smoking. Your aunt couldn't have children. It comes from YOUR side of the family - Darko's fine."

"Darko, I don't want to see her either. Keep her away from me."

Heartless, -- they're heartless. How could this be happening? It's all a bad dream. It MUST be. Why hasn't a doctor come to talk to me? This was becoming a horror story.

December 12th -- a.m.

Dr. Moore, a sweet, motherly, well-groomed lady, was finally standing by my bed, choking back tears, at a loss for words. Very tenderly she said, "Dr. Glupa, a specialist, is coming to speak to you. These things happen. They can't be helped. Women have three, six, even ten babies and then one with spina bifida. It's not hereditary. You have less chance now of having another S.B. baby than anyone else. She'll explain." Not wanting to show the tears in her eyes, she left.

I sat dazed. Am I in shock? None of this is registering. Everything will be all right. It has to be! I'll take a shower. Maybe I'll wake up in my bedroom, still pregnant.

While standing in the shower, letting the water roll down my flabby body, a head appeared, "Would you turn off the tap, please. I'm in a hurry."

I was embarrassed. What was she doing, intruding into my meager privacy? I didn't mind people staring at my anatomy while I was pregnant, but I didn't have that excuse now, it was just jiggly flesh.

"I'm the specialist, Dr. Glupa. Your child won't live more than a few weeks. Her head will enlarge from the spinal fluids and she'll be paralyzed from the waist down. If she possibly lives longer, she'll be blind and the growth will get larger. You'll have to put her in a home, she'll need round the clock attention. I'm late for an appointment. Sorry."

The head was gone. It vanished as quickly as it had appeared. I don't know how long I stood there with the water turned off, trying to decipher what had just happened and what this dark haired head had just said. No emotion -- she could have been talking about the muffler of my car at a garage.

Back in my room, 'I' was emotionless. I couldn't cry, just stare. A woman walked in. "I'm the head nurse of this floor. You'll have to put your baby in a home. She can't stay here. She's in a 'newborn' nursery, for healthy babies. Make arrangements."

"Where?" I gasped. "Why didn't she have surgery? We've inquired and in most other countries they would have operated till she was either normal or dead. How can you just leave her like that -- to die?"

"I don't know why, I just know you both have to leave this hospital, tomorrow."

"Why can't I just take her home?"

"She needs professional and special attention that you couldn't give her."

She was right. I was hoping against hope somebody had misdiagnosed. This was no longer a hole the size of a quarter. Her body was growing out of the opening.

"Can you find an institution for us to put her in?" I asked thinking realistically once again.

"No, in Ontario, babies have to be two years old to be institutionalized. She won't live that long", she replied, still businesslike and callused, bombarding answers.

"What do I do with her till then?" I choked back tears now.

"I don't know. You had her. She's your problem, not ours. If you can't hack it, there's the window -- JUMP!

If I wasn't utterly paralyzed from the cold abruptness of this woman, I would have lunged for her throat. This was a nurse? They were supposed to serve and protect, or something like that. Didn't they take an oath of humanity, dedication or something? My mind couldn't digest medical terminology. She's telling me to end my problem by ending my life. I was past the point of furious. Adrenaline pumping, I picked up the phone. Sue the nurses, sue the doctors, sue the hospital, they can't do this to me. (Years later I found that this lady had acted the villain in kindness. She shocked me back to reality by diverting my anger and frustration and directing it at her so I would not succumb to self pity and sit and vegetate. Instead she knew I'd take the situation by the horns and start reacting to life.)

The following day the Health Minister of Ontario had arranged to have my baby placed in an old age home in Whitby, which had facilities for small babies with birth defects. I would have to transport her there myself. Could I really handle that? The good thing was, it meant I'd be able to hold her for a few hours - actually hold her!

I must make arrangement to have her baptized immediately. Why hadn't I thought of that before? I'll have to find a priest to come to the hospital in the morning. Who? Can't get the priest who married us; he'd wonder why he hadn't seen us since. The hospital must have one for emergencies. Darko's sister can be the godmother.

"Mr. and Mrs. Martonfi, by what name shall I christen the baby?"

I don't know. I haven't thought of any girls' names. The only one I like is Michelle, but if she's not going to live, I don't want to waste the name. "Both our names start with a 'D' so, let's call her Diana."

'Waste' a name? What was I thinking? I'd become a monster.

I left the hospital without my baby. At home, neither Darko nor I could take down the crib. That would be too final. "Maybe tomorrow she'd be okay and come home," our numbed minds rationalized. When I returned to take her to Whitby, my precious bundle was brought to me to be dressed for her long journey. My words haunted me, "I don't want to waste the name!??" How cruel. I'm as heartless as those around me. 'I' was going to be a good mother? How could such a thought enter my head? This tiny angel deserved the best in the short time allotted her. She wasn't a waste. What's happening to me? Am I becoming a mechanical robot? My heart was breaking. In a few hours she would be miles away, laying helplessly, waiting to die -- in an old age home. I would never call another child Michelle - ever. Will I be able to live through this?

My dad drove us to Whitby, in one of the worst snow storms we'd seen in many years. On one bridge we thought we wouldn't make it through the drifts. I feared we'd be stranded for hours. Could she live without an incubator for that long? "Please God, don't let her die here in my arms." That I couldn't handle. Upon arriving, I couldn't muster enough courage to walk through the home. It was the saddest place I had ever seen. I thought I had seen all aspects of life in my nineteen years -- but I'd never been exposed to something like this. So many, old and young, on the brink of death. It was all too heartbreaking, too wrenching. Dad and I both cried. Odd, I thought my dad couldn't cry. Only my mother CRIES. We started for home in silence.

"Good-bye little darling, I love you."

Darko was home by the time I reached the apartment. My dad made his apologies for not coming up. The crib, still beside my bed, screamed of its emptiness.

I wanted a baby - any baby. Today! Now! Please! Somebody help me! I'm just aching. A husband cannot fulfill that ache. Only a baby could.

Tossing for hours, not able to sleep, staring at the empty crib in the dark, I rose from bed and went and curled up on the sofa. Angry now, I lashed out at God. "GOD, are you up there? Can you hear me? What have I ever done to You to deserve this? You knew how we wanted a baby! You knew how we planned to give our child the best in life. There are people out there having babies that don't want babies. Giving them away! Normal babies. WHY ME? WHY DID YOU DO THIS TO ME?" I was almost yelling, but when I had stopped, I sensed this overwhelming peace. It was unbelievable, I could almost touch it. IT WAS GOD! I heard distinctly;

"I DIDN'T DO THIS BUT I WILL SHOW YOU HOW GREAT I AM, I WILL SEND YOU
TWIN BOYS. I WILL REPAY, SAYS THE LORD GOD."

Chapter Two

A LITTLE BIT O´ HAPPINESS

"Darko! DARKO! Wake up! We´re going to have twins. Boys! GOD JUST TOLD ME!"

Groggy from only a couple of hours of rest, my sleepy husband put his arms around me and said, "This has all been too much for you. Go to sleep. You need some rest. I should have gone with you today. I couldn´t get more time off. I´m sorry."

"Didn´t you HEAR what I just said? GOD just spoke to me in the living room. He told me we´re going to have twins!"

"Yes, okay. Get some rest."

There was no use pursuing this. To Darko, believing in God was like believing in Santa Claus. Coming from a country behind the iron curtain, he thought God was for little kids and very, very old women, or for people who needed a crutch; definitely not for him. In the morning, I leaped (not at all like me) out of bed and rushed to phone a ´chosen few´ with my astonishing good news.

All responded the same way. "Get some rest. You´ve gone through an ordeal. Everything will be all right. Don´t take it so hard."

Why doesn´t anyone out there believe God can talk? Surely if He could make us, He could talk to us. I was convinced He could. He DID - TO ME!

Months passed and Diana´s condition deteriorated. Her tiny body stayed the same size, but the growth on her back grew larger than she was herself. I built an invisible wall. I could not allow myself to get attached to her. It hurt too much. I couldn´t look at ANY small child.

Day by day, whenever the phone rang, I feared it was the home calling saying she had died. Fearful -- yet desperately wanting to be able to mourn my loss. You can only mourn for the dead -- not the living. My emotions and feelings were mixed in sheer turmoil. You bury the dead, mourn the loss, then continue with the business of living. In my dilemma I found I was mourning for ME -- NOT HER.

Darko and I had moved into our newly built home. Bills, bills, bills; mortgages, hydro, water, telephone and insurance bills. All were piling up, higher than we could imagine possible. The real estate agent had never discussed anything other than the cost of the mortgage payments. We also hadn't bargained on the GO train which went through our backyard every thirty minutes. He failed to mention this little feature when he sold us that house in the dark cover of the night. We hadn't anticipated these many extras.

We decided the only way we could buy groceries and buy furniture for this three bedroom home was to start our own business. I was once again thoroughly disgusted with the company I worked for. Keypunching and only keypunching was not as rewarding as I had thought. I definitely needed a rest after my last job, but I was soon bored. When a new position became available, I applied with seven others to be a Data Processing Manager. (I was working for a large Toronto bakery). The position would go to the one who got the highest marks on the exam they had scheduled. I, along with six men, spent three days writing exams. "PIECE OF CAKE." Data Processing was my best subject. I tied for first place. My superior took me aside to explain why the position was going to the 'man'. I would be having children, diapers, etc. They wanted someone who would give his 'all' to the company. "Are you certain you didn't shave off a mark or two on my papers, maybe?"

"How could you think such a thing?"

"Then why did you even let me compete to get the advancement?"

"I really didn't think you had the know-how." was his only reply.

"SEE YOU, BYE!"

We began our new business by driving along the main streets of Toronto after dark and noting all the neon signs that needed repair. During 'working hours', I would call the various establishments, our prospective clients, and inform them that our observant night patrolman had noticed their sign was defective and not a reflection of their professional image. It worked! We were in business. Still impoverished, but none-the-less, in BUSINESS!

We traded our lovely sports car, as much as it hurt, for a ¾ ton truck, a ladder and boxes of screwdrivers, and we turned a new page in our lives.

I longed to get pregnant! I learned that the 'rhythm method' also worked in reverse. I'd try any short cut. Each morning before rising, I anxiously took my temperature. Unfortunately -- normal readings. No babies. No twins. Then I'd move to the floor in the third bedroom and canvas for business till Darko got home. Only a phone and a pillow, and oh yes, a large ashtray, but it was our 'executive office'. We were businessmen. I was Manager, Secretary and Bookkeeper. Prince Charming was President, Vice-president, Master Electrician and Bill Collector. IF these giant corporations could only see me sitting there on the floor, pretending to have a staff of dozens, they wouldn't have given me the time of day. Rather than hire a journeyman, who we couldn't afford, I would have to play apprentice many times and hold the ladder for Darko in the middle of busy streets, directing traffic around the ladder. Sometimes, I'd pass material and tools up to him so he'd save time and not have to climb up and down so many times.

These were the days before women's lib. We really DID STOP traffic. I never went out of the house without four inch spike heels and a beehive hairdo. WHAT A PAIR!

By the spring of '68 we had built up our business to a twenty-four hour around the clock emergency service. Industrial, commercial, and residential; weekends, holidays, Dominion Day, -- EVERYDAY. When Darko wasn't sleeping, he was working. This hectic schedule left precious little time to drive me back and forth to Whitby. Having no transportation meant having to ask close family members for rides. Not many were willing to spend an afternoon in an old age home. I couldn't blame most of them. I did blame my in-laws though. My father-in-law, prematurely retired, had wheels. He didn't put 200 miles a year on that car. In thirty years it would still be brand new. What a waste. My mother-in-law wouldn't even acknowledge she had a grandchild, much less go see her. Her attitude? Looking at a blind person could make you go blind -- so who knows the consequences of visiting 'HER'. I truly felt I understood. Coming from the background she did; her upbringing was full of primitive old wives' tales. I almost EXPECTED this attitude.

Her love for me had completely died in one short day, back when Darko and I returned from our New York honeymoon.

"Why aren't you coming to MY house for dinner? I have it all prepared."

Surprised that Darko's mother was screaming through the phone, I half apologized, "We had it arranged that we would eat at my mom's, and then pick up the rest of Darko's belongings, and move them to the apartment. We'll be there for supper, if you like. I wasn't asked or told to come for lunch, I'm sorry you went to all the trouble."

We arrived about 7:00 p.m. As soon as the front door opened we were greeted with, "It's about time you thought of us and not just your parents." The icicles hung off each word.

"My dad picked us up at the airport and we couldn't ask him to drive us here first, especially since we had previously arranged for my mother to make lunch." What was she starting?

Before we were even seated, I was taken aback by her comment. No, it was more a statement. "Darko, tell 'Dana' to write us a check for $7,000.00. We're going to buy a duplex. You're going to live upstairs; we're going to live downstairs. We're putting the house in our name so when we die we'll leave it to you. Don't worry, you'll have your privacy, but you'll both have to stop smoking." All this was said in one breath.

Amazing! When had she planned all THIS? She must be kidding. Yes, we did receive $7,000 as cash gifts, but the liquor and wine bill came to $2,200. The wedding albums would cost $900 and our honeymoon was more than $1,000. The T.V.-stereo another $1,000. We had less than $2,000 left for necessities such as a kitchen table, chairs, a sofa, a rug and maybe even a coffee table.

"You've known for weeks that we have leased the apartment for one year. We have also discussed the fact that we are never going to live with either you OR my parents." I was trying to keep my voice calm. The nerve!

"It´s a stupid idea, an apartment. Such a waste of money. WE´VE been looking with a real estate agent all this week and WE´VE decided WE´RE (meaning them and us) buying a duplex!", she retorted.

"Well you go right ahead, but not with US you´re not!" I responded in disbelief. My voice wasn´t loud or disrespectful, just firm.

Glaring at me indignantly she just continued, "We´re old. My son can´t just drop us like this. What will we do?"

"COME OFF IT!" Now my voice was loud. "You´re not old, you´re only forty-three! You´ve had Darko´s paycheck for three and a half years and now you´ll just have to do without it. He´s given you a GOOD start. Now we have to start saving for OUR future and OUR old age and HIS and MY family."

"You´ll see when you´re a mother. Three days I screamed in pain giving birth to him. This is the thanks I get? God´s going to punish you, you´ll see."

Darko just stared, saying nothing, as if he couldn´t see either of us. "Say something!", I thought. "Anything. Just don´t tell her we don´t have $7,000, then we'd really be in trouble, squandering all that money."

A short time later, we said our goodnights. "I didn´t think you were such a witch, Dana," she whimpered, tears streaming down her face. My face was set with a cock-eyed, stunned expression, which I was certain was embedding wrinkles two inches deep, if not turning my hair gray.

Our first evening in our unfurnished nest was ruined. "Why didn´t you say something back to your mother?"

"Ignore her like I do. She'll get the message."

"She called me a witch. I was polite, I wasn't rude or disrespectful." I would have been if I could express my feelings better in Croatian. I get tongue-tied.

"You should have just told her we didn't have the $7,000."

"She wouldn't have believe me." I could feel my blood pressure rising. I was shaking. "Me! A WITCH! After years of catering to her every whim. I'M A WITCH?" Now I could think of oodles of comebacks, in both languages.

"You're a beautiful witch, forget it."

Looking back to that day, I could see a distinct curtain being drawn in my relationship with my mother-in-law that had never been there before. This would continue for many, many years. I took her son! I wasn't going to give him back! The nerve of me!

Darko charged through our front door excitedly, "Come see what I just bought you. You'll love it! You'll be able to drive yourself to Whitby and see Diana any time you want."

"Oh-h-h, it must be a car! You got me a car! I'm thrilled!!"

Now standing outside I asked, quite puzzled, "What is that, Darko?"

"It's a Peugot."

"Looks more like a pigeon. Am I going to fit in it? Is it safe ---"

"Sure as long as you don't try to put your feet on the floor."

"Darko, THE FLOOR'S MISSING!"

"That's okay, it's okay. You won't fall out. Look at it this way, you won't need air conditioning."

"It doesn't have side mirrors OR windshield wipers. I can't drive without side mirrors."

"Sure you can, but I'll have to get you windshield wipers. I'll fix it up."

"How much did it cost, Darko?"

"Ninety bucks. A real bargain -- We'll fix it up and get two hundred for it easy."

As it later turned out, I made over 30,000 miles on my pigeon and did sell it for $200.00. That's another story, which started a long list of buying and selling cars at a marginal profit, each time working up to a bigger and better car.

Summer 1968

Mom and dad had been running a variety store for just over a year. During the summer evenings, Darko and I would go to the store, hang around or play cards with my dad; our favorite passtime, and cheap entertainment.

July 16th, 1968

The phone ringing could hardly be heard over the clamour of our card game.

"Donna, it's for you," my mother said half surprised. "Who would know that you're here?"

I knew who would. I had left all the numbers where I could be reached with the home in Whitby.

"Mrs. Martonfi, your daughter's condition has worsened."

"Should I come right now?" My heart skipped beats.

"No, no, there is nothing you can do. Will you be at this number much longer?"

"Probably until midnight."

"We'll call if there is any change."

11:35 p.m.

The ringing cut through the silence of four people staring blankly into space. IT was inevitable. She was already more than eight months old. She fought for life much longer than anyone had anticipated.

"Mrs. Martonfi, your little girl just passed away quietly. She didn´t suffer nor was she in pain. Bless her heart. Would you notify us when you´ve made the funeral arrangements?"

Was I relieved she had passed away? Possibly, but Seeing her body becoming more and more deformed as the weeks passed was more than words could express. She felt no pain but I couldn´t imagine something that looked so RAW not being painful.

She´s in a better place now, thank God. She's a little angel, in heaven. I had to believe that. How else could I cope? How else could I look forward to my TWINS and attempt a life of happiness?

To this day, the funeral is a hazy blurred image of people crying over a tiny white coffin. Why are they crying? Now? They should have cried when she was born - not now. She´s in God´s hands now.

"Dana, the very next long weekend we´ll pack a picnic lunch, some blankets and drive to the cemetery for the day." Until this statement, I thought mom-in-law had already shocked, mortified, and stunned me more than anyone ever could.

"I´m not going to a cemetery, for a picnic!", I stormed back. "Why didn´t you want to see her when she was alive? Now you think we´re going to have a family gathering, a standing date, at a cemetery?"

"We have to pick a name plate for her." she replied, camouflaging her previous macabre statement, pretending to have been misunderstood.

"We can't afford a name plate just now. There's time for that. I'll know where she is without a marker."

"Dana, you are so mean and cruel, you don't deserve children." she replied.

The first long weekend after the funeral, Darko and I found ourselves, at the insistence of his parents, standing over a tiny grave with this inscription:

DIHJANNE MARTONFI
    December 7, 1967 - July 16, 1968

D-I-H-J-A-N-N-E???

"Isn't this a nice surprise, Dana? I picked it out myself. Paid for it, too."

"Why couldn't you spell her name right?" My voice was hardly audible from the strain.

"It doesn't matter how I spelled it. I PAID FOR IT!"

"How did you manage then to get the last name correct? Is it just a problem you have with first names?" I was really beginning to hate this woman. Did she do it on purpose? I didn't mind her not knowing how to spell my name after more than five years, but this was inexcusable. "GET OUT OF MY LIFE", my mind screamed. "Just stay away from me!"

An excited, familiar voice came blurting through the phone, "Donna, Paul and I are moving to Grimsby. Could you and Darko lend us a hand?" It was Anna, one of the high school gang. She was bubbly, energetic and fun-loving. I related to Anna because she had recently lost her first baby to crib death. She had come through her tragedy with no visible scars, and was now pregnant again. If she could make it -- I could too. I had twins to look forward to.

"Sure, Anna, we'd be happy to."

"Steve and Millie are coming and we´ll make a fun weekend of it. Pizza, Chinese food, eat, drink, the 'woiks'. You´ll have to sleep on the floor in sleeping bags -- bring your funny thermometer. Are you still trying or has something taken root?"

"Nothing yet. Do you think maybe I should be using two thermometers?"

"Listen, you´d be the first person I know to sense the fluttering of a new life the morning of its conception."

"Lives, Anna, lives. Plural, THINK PLURAL."

The six of us were like a comedy team from an old Laurel and Hardy movie. Horsing around, joking, being silly. If you can imagine, me in my pigeon, crammed with clothes and household goods, all the way to Grimsby? I was relaxing and really unwinding with not an immediate care in the world, except for the probability of this car actually making the trip.

I realized that this was the crucial, mid-month, ´try for twins´ cycle, most conducive for getting pregnant. In the privacy of my own heart, and according to my thermometer, the miracle of conception was possible. God´s promise -- possibly this month.

Upon awakening, stiff from the hard floor, I mechanically reached for my thermometer, as I had repeatedly done many mornings before. This time, I was jolted awake, probably the first and only time in my entire life. I am NOT a morning person except THIS morning. Where´s Darko?

"Darko, Darko, Honey!" I was now pounding on the bathroom door. "This is it! It registered BELOW normal!" Gasping between breaths, "I´m pregnant! WE´RE PREGNANT! We´re having our twins!"

I knew that if I was up, certainly EVERYONE else was up. I zoomed downstairs, feet touching every third step, babbling, "I´m pregnant, I´m pregnant! I´m having TWINS."

All gawked at me like I had just given birth upstairs to six ducks and came down wearing two heads.

"Good for you," Paul muttered.

MEN!

My mind raced into the future. First thing Monday morning, I have to phone Dr. Moore and tell her I'm pregnant and arrange for appointments. She'll be so thrilled. I sensed a special doctor-patient relationship with her. She'd become a part-time mother hen, encouraging me, explaining why it's harder to become pregnant when you're overly anxious.

I was past the point of anxious. Desperate was more the word. Desperate for a baby to hold in my arms and rock to sleep. I'll have to get a wooden rocker - tenderly, gently, rocking. Too bad I already have one crib. I heard that the large department stores would give you an additional crib if you delivered twins and had bought well in advance of knowing that you needed two.

Doctor Moore's gentle face showed a trace of concern. "Now let's just take one step at a time. We won't know for certain for some time yet. We'll wait till you miss your period."

I didn't miss any periods with my other pregnancy. "Do you think it was because she wasn't normal?"

"We don't know at this point." Her voice was gentle and soothing.

"If you have a showing, it doesn't necessarily mean anything is wrong with the baby."

"BABIES, Dr. Moore, BABIES!" I corrected.

Lovingly, yet firmly, she replied, "Don't do this to yourself, Donna, twins do not run in your family. Don't build your hopes to the point of being disappointed with only ONE baby. Let's just concentrate on one healthy, bouncing baby, for now."

She just didn't understand.

"Don't take any medication whatsoever, not even an aspirin. If you have a headache -- then have a headache. NO PILLS."

"What about my smoking? I chain smoke, you know."
Everybody chain smokes these days.

"Your anxiety would cause more harm to the child if you quit now than the nicotine would. I know better than to advise you to quit. I definitely suggest however that you cut down to a bare minimum.

In the months that followed, my feet hardly touched the ground. Even with monthly spotting, I knew that God wouldn't send me two babies to turn around and take them both away from me. He's just not that kind of God.

Even with my very few close friends, like Anna, I couldn't share my innermost feelings and thoughts. They couldn't comprehend GOD, let alone whether He was up there talking to anyone. 'It just doesn't happen.' Relatives, aunts and neighbors were even worse.

"How could you get pregnant again?"

"Why would you risk bringing another crippled child into this world?"

"Aren't you frightened that IT'S not normal?"

My mother just cried. I didn't know whether out of joy or grief, because she's always crying. Other people breathe, my mother cries.

No, I wasn't frightened. I had a peace about this pregnancy. A peace about my soon to be born sons. I knew deep, deep inside that God was in control, though I often wondered why He wasn't the first time.

By June I was literally as big as a barn. A stranger at a plaza stopped and asked if I would be offended if he took a picture of my side profile. "Offended? I'd be honored. If you knew what it took to get this size." Nothing short of God Himself, I almost added.

From the rear, I had a waistline. Starting at about where your arms hang, at the side, I jetted out as if I had a concealed television set under my dress, including hi-fi speakers. I noticed, many times after, camera buffs clicking away as I waddled past.

It was in this humungous condition, sprawled on a lawn chair, soaking up the sun (if I had to be big, I didn't have to look like a mountain of cheese) that I met Sharon, soon to become a lifelong friend. Walking directly toward where I was laying, she impressed me with a gentleness and grace that made her unique. Tall and slender, she had a warm smile that was only matched by her height. When she got within hearing range, she proclaimed, "I live only a few doors away. How far along are you?"

"Hello," I tried to sit up, "I'm just barely six months."

"Wow! Are YOU EVER BIG! I'm pregnant too, into my fifth month."

"You are not," I blurted, before realizing what I was saying and tried muttering an apology.

"Oh listen, don't apologize, my baby has enough room to stand up straight in there."

I liked her immediately. Thorough the course of the afternoon, I discovered that she was a nurse, originally from Saskatchewan, living a few doors away among seven relatives (all from her husband's side); going through a drastic time -- absolute culture shock.

"What a relief to meet someone who's not Portuguese. Ninety-nine percent of the people on this block are Portuguese. My mother-in-law can't figure out why ONLY you and your husband live in this three bedroom house. She's trying to get four more relatives to move in with us and fill up the basement. She's been watching you from behind the curtains in the living room. Everyone peeks from behind curtains around here. I'm going to go insane. I want to move away so-o-o bad. The seven of them, plus hubby, baby and I, makes TEN."

It was obvious from the overflowing, unsolicited conversation, this gal needed companionship as badly as I did.

"I can just tell we're going to be the best of friends. We've got a very common problem." I joked.

"What? Our babies?", was her obvious conclusion.

"No," I laughed, "our mothers-in-law."

Exchanging stories I learned she'd been married for eight years and many doctors had told her she would never be able to conceive.

"Surprise, surprise! It might be small, it might be standing up, but there's definitely somebody kicking in there!"

The gaiety of the moment was interrupted when Sharon spotted a dead pigeon by the side of my house. "That's supposed to be a bad omen, you know." I noticed a frown cross her face.

"I wish they'd all roll over and drop dead," I proceeded, "I can't hang my wash outside without re-washing a good portion of it."

Her frown changed to a sheepish grin, "We have a pigeon coop with thirty-four homers. They sometimes fly till they drop from exhaustion. There should be a law. I swear my mother-in-law cooks them. I never eat chicken over there, just in case."

"YUK. Only pigeon I want to see around here is the one parked in my driveway."

With the weekend looming ahead of me like a dark cloud on a sunny day, having a friend that could relate to having an insensitive mother-in-law, became invaluable.

We were invited for Sunday dinner, by you can guess who. Seated beside mom-in-law on the sofa, she raised both her arms to the top of her head, leaned back and said matter of factly, "This baby isn't going to be normal either because you're smoking too much." (I have never smoked in her presence) "I'm concerned. The smell of smoke bothers babies. You don't deserve children anyway. They're all going to be deformed because of the way you've treated me."

My face crimson, my fists clenched, I gasped, "TREATED YOU?"

"Taking my son. I'm not allowed to see him. When I think of the three days I spent in labor with him, sheer agony. I almost died."

"NOT ALLOWED TO SEE YOUR SON" I retorted. "You see him every Sunday."

"I need an appointment, though," wailing through the tears. I had seen those tears before. She could turn them on and off like a tap.

"YOU have no concern for this baby or what bothers him -- otherwise you'd lower your arms because YOUR odor offends anyone within five feet of you. As for your son -- you only care about his paycheck."

WOW! That was strong stuff, even for me, but she had just cursed my babies. My 'in-laws' just became my 'out-laws'. Dad-in-law, never saying more than hello and good-bye, was now rising to his feet, proclaiming sharply; "If you're going to upset Mama like this, you're not welcomed in our house anymore."

Sheer relief flooded through my body. The facade was down. I wouldn't have to be subjected to these, 'ROAST DANA' Sunday dinners anymore. IT was their decision, not mine. In my condition I didn't know how many more weekends like this I could tolerate without becoming physically violent. Why had I put up with it for so long?

"Sharon, guess what! Good news! I don't have to be roasted by my out-laws ever again. They just threw me out! I'm planning a celebration for next Sunday, you're invited. DON'T YOU DARE BRING YOURS, you hear?"

It was an act, a put on. I was still trembling. When did she turn into such a hateful battle-ax? Was it because I didn't call her MAMA like she had wanted? I didn't even call my own mother Mama. I'd called her and my dad by their first names until I was three years old. My grandmother had raised me till then.

After we came to Canada, I spent over a year being raised by a great-aunt. One day she stuck my head in the oven and set my hair on fire. That was an accident, because she was merely trying to dry my hair, but I was still greatly traumatized. She would also tie me to a chair, every night for over a year, so that I couldn´t get up until my homework was done. Once, she hit me so hard that the chair and I tumbled down a flight of stairs. The mention of her name terrifies me to this day.

I´ve called no one MAMA and I wasn´t about to start now

Chapter Three

MIRACLE ... PROBABLY A FIGMENT OF YOUR IMAGINATION

The July heat didn't bother me at all, but I worried that the end of August would be a hard time to give birth.

Doctor Moore's office was never overly crowded, so I'd be in and out in a few minutes. The secretary called out, "Mrs. Martonfi, Dr. Moore would also like to see your husband this time." Why would she want to see him, I wondered?

"Is anything wrong?"

Dr. Moore appeared in the door, "No, no, no Donna. Just wanted to stress to Darko the importance of him talking you out of the idea that you're having TWINS." She continued, "There's only one baby, one very large baby. ONE heart beat. ONLY ONE."

I couldn't accept that. Darko was now interjecting, "You know something doctor, I'm beginning to actually believe her. Not only has this idea kept her from worrying about this pregnancy -- I haven't worried. Couldn't you send her for an X-ray?"

"If that's what it'll take to convince both of you, okay. I'll make out the requisition and you can go over there right now. Prepare yourself for a letdown, better now than in the delivery room."

I could hardly breathe. In a few minutes I would know, for sure. "Drive faster, faster, Darko."

We sat looking at each other in wonderment, anticipation, expectation and fear.

"Okay. You may go now," interrupted the technician.

"GO? But -- but -- "How many are there?"

"How many? Wait and I'll look." It was the longest wait of my life. Coming back, she nonchalantly said, "Oh, there's two."

TWO! T-W-O!

"Please, could I see?"

"I don't know what you're going to see, but come on in."

Barely able to see through tears, I gazed upon the most incredible sight; "They're -- beautiful."

"No, no those are your hip bones. This is ONE head," she pointed, "and there's the other -- already in the birth canal."

"They're certainly larger than my hip bones. Aren't they?"

She seemed to be surprised that anyone could be so naive.

I rushed to Darko. We hugged, we kissed, we jumped up and down. The people in the halls and elevator must have wondered if we had just now learned of my condition, which was more than obvious to them.

"SHARON, ANNA, EVERYBODY! I TOLD YOU SO!" Talk about my feet not touching the ground -- I had sprouted wings and was flying.

Sharon was outside, within yelling distance, as we pulled into the driveway. "Oh Sharon, it's true. It's true, I saw them."

"THEM?" She threw her arms around my neck (not that easy a task, across two bellies). Wiping tears away, "Well I guess I can forgive you."

"Forgive me? For what?" I asked.

"Remember yesterday when I was slopping my dinner all over myself, trying to get it to my mouth...?"

"Yeah?"

"I was so angry -- there you were sitting nice and comfy, your plate, knife, fork, napkin, even drink -- all perched on top of your stomach, WITHOUT EVEN A TRAY!" We were almost rolling in the street with laughter.

"Oh-h-h stop -- stop -- my bladder isn´t what it used to be."

"You don´t have any room in there for a bladder. What BLADDER?"

Darko was calling from the kitchen window, "Telephone!"

Trying to hurry, I heard the smart aleck, "Dr. Moore, it takes her more than just a minute or two to get from the doorstep to the door, be patient."

She was going on and on about taking it easy. According to the X-rays, I had started to dilate. It would be just a bit too early-- they seemed small. "Promise to stay in bed or I´ll put you in the hospital. By the way, Donna, I cannot tell you how overwhelmed I am. Speechless actually. I couldn´t think of anyone I would rather see happy than the two of you. Take care, dear." What a sweetheart. I loved this lady.

About three days off my feet was more than tiring. "Sharon, let´s go to the park, I have to find a breeze." It was hot, too. I could get air conditioning in my ´pigeon´, but the HOUSE had NO holes in the floor.,

"We´d better take the fellas along. It would take both of them to carry you home if something should happen."

That night I could only get comfortable on the floor under the bedroom window. About 4:30 a.m. I woke absolutely soaking wet. WET! "Darko, get on the phone, my water broke."

Typical husband -- jumped twelve feet in the air -- "WHAT´S BROKEN?"

"It´s okay. It´s supposed to break, dummy."

Well, if Dr. "M" could be so nonchalant about waiting till nine a.m. I guess there was no panic. "Darko go back to sleep, you´ve got ´til nine."

Hmmm -- 5:00 a.m. Wonder if I should call Sharon? I'm going to wake up at least nine people. S-u-u-r-r-e, why not? This is my big day.

"Hello? Sharon? Do you want to come over for a cup of coffee?"

I could hear her -- not through the phone -- she was at the front door, trying to break in. I hadn't even finished talking. Poor Sharon was all out of breath and almost knocked me over as I opened the door. "Did you call an ambulance?!"

"Why would you think I needed an ambulance, I merely invited you in for coffee?"

"Donna, stop joking. You wouldn't call at 5:00 a.m. unless THIS WAS IT."

"It is, but I have no pains -- nothing."

"By nine o'clock we're going to need a sump-pump. No wonder I'm so big. Did you ever see so much water?"

By 7:30 we decided I should let my mom and dad in on the fun. They lived six minutes away (by car). They were at the front door in three.

"R u krazy? U vant to hav dem here?"

"Dad, where are your teeth? You can't talk. Go get your teeth." Mom joined in the commotion, "Never mind his teeth -- someone call the ambulance."

Everyone was moving or pacing, here, there, everywhere. It didn't take long to persuade me that I should go by ambulance. It was the fastest way to get away from all this fuss. Now the attendant's asking if I need help. "No, I'm fine, I'll walk. I'm going to have twins!" I boasted.

"Only TWINS? I would have thought there were at least five in there." Finally someone with a sense of humor. Darko, my parents, even Sharon, were half hysterical.

I heard Sharon yell out to my dad, "Daj pusu." A phrase she thought meant "good-bye", because she had heard me say it many times to Darko over the phone. If my dad hadn't forgotten his teeth, he would have lost them there and then. 'Daj pusu' means; 'give me a kiss'.

9:30 That Evening

I was starving. If they wouldn't feed me, at least they let me smoke. My stomach had reduced to half the size of when I came in. Gallons of water had flushed out, but, still no labor pains.

"Mr. Martonfi, you look tired," a nurse directed her comments toward where he was lying in the next bed. "why don't you go home? She's not ready. Could even be tomorrow."

"Yes Darko, go. I'll be fine. I'm in great shape now that the second heartbeat has been detected. Go on home." (Their little hearts had been beating simultaneously).

"Okay mum, but they have to call me the minute you have your first pain." With that, he left.

"Nurse!" Something had only now come to mind. Something I'd tried to block out. "What day of the month is it?"

"Why, ummm, it's July sixteenth."

JULY SIXTEENTH ... OH, -- if they could only come tonight. Not tomorrow. Tonight. OH GLORY! This was so appropriate. God repaying two on the same day He took Diana. We would never mourn the day she died; instead, we'd mourn the day of her birth, December the seventh.

"Nurse, then you'd better catch my husband, I've just started labor."

Not very much later, I'm inquiring, "Where's my epidural?"

"Oh you don't get one with twins. We'd have problems with the second baby." I hardly recognized her in this get-up. "Is it bad?" Dr. 'M' asked.

"No, but if I can't have an epidural, then you better run and get my cigarettes .... By the way, I've been meaning to show you something, doctor."

"Is she kidding? What did you let her bring IN HERE?"

Half in panic, a nurse was apologizing, "Nothing, NOTHING!"

"No, no, it's on my neck." I said, pointing. "Since I'm here, could you remove this large cyst? I grow them all the time." I was completely serious. "The last time I had one removed, in this same spot, they went and lost it."

All the laughter and calamity that erupted attracted Darko's curiosity from the hall. "This sounds more like a wild party! What's going on in there?"

"Out! GET OUT! Stay out in the hall. Here comes the first head -- yes -- yes -- push once more."

A baby's cry penetrated the room.

"Is it all right? Dr. Moore, IS IT ALL RIGHT?"

"Yes, yes, 'Baby Boy A' is fine. Lay back, push again."

In my insurmountable relief I relaxed against the bed, searching the room for a clock. 11:35 p.m. Baby Boy 'A' made it. Still on July 16th. 11:35!!

"Push Donna, come on -- you don't want them to have separate birth days. Push."

'Baby Boy B' checked into the world at 11:42. Neither words, nor pen and paper could capture what was in my heart. Healthy. Both perfect. I tried desperately to focus through the tears at these two precious gifts. Laying side by side, 'A' screaming to let the world know he arrived; 'B', one leg dangling over the side of the bin, yawning, looked like he was wondering why this other fellow was making such a racket, keeping him awake. This one's going to be like DADDY.

To a young mother who was apprehensive about her babies' state of health in the first place, some very commonplace things that happened, ended up being terrifying incidents. About the third night after my delivery, a nurse over anxiously rushed to the side of my bed asking if I could contact my husband right away. I almost fell off my bed. My instant reaction was that one had died. "No. No. Your husband´s been calling and the switchboard disconnected him twice. He must be furious." I was furious! Couldn´t she think?

Day four: While ´daddy´ and I were standing at the nursery window, a nurse walked to the incubator of ´Baby Boy B´, took him out, and proceeded to insert a tube down his throat. I collapsed on the floor. He must have stopped breathing! "No, no, that was a gavage. Their sucking instincts hadn´t fully developed. It is much faster and easier to pour the milk into their stomachs."

When other moms were resting, I was at the nursery window, my eyes fixed on the two incubators. The palms of my hands shot to the window as I watched a stream of water shoot out from my baby onto the incubator glass.

"My baby´s sprung a leak in his side!" My heart and emotions had bypassed logic. My daughter had a hole in her back and now I had reasoned that he was imperfect too. Fortunately, I was unaccustomed to little boys. Little boys in oversized diapers.

By the time I left the hospital, I needed a hospital. I was a nervous wreck. When would my mind accept the fact that they were healthy? Tiny, but A okay! I was more than happy to leave the hospital though, even if I had to leave them behind so that they could gain some weight, before being brought home.

The world was in a tizzy about three astronauts landing on the moon, on this same July 16th. Big deal, I´m not impressed.

Takes a lot more than that to impress this mommy. Imagine taking the limelight away from my boys. Some good is bound to come of this lunar landing -- one astronaut´s name was Michael. MICHAEL. Michael Martonfi. I like that! Perfect, as a matter of fact, especially since I felt he was sent from ´outer space´.

Always planning to call my first son Daniel, baby boy ´A´ became Daniel and baby boy ´B´ became astronaut Michael.

I would have thought Martonfi would be hard to match up. Darko, Donna, Diana, Daniel --- Michael? Would he mind not starting with a ´D´? No, of course not, he´ll be the only one out of the lot they´ll be able to find in the phone book. Anyway, you can´t have two DOCTOR D. MARTONFI, M.D.´s.

Chapter Four

HAPPY ... WOULDN´T YOU BE

Boy! Did we have a lot of acquaintances! I didn´t recall knowing half of these people! I felt like I was in a side show. Every semi-stranger that appeared at my door was accompanied by at least two of his third cousins.

"Mother, you cannot parade all these people through my house at all hours of the day and night." My parents closed their store at 10:00 p.m. and then wanted to socialize. In her pride and excitement she stopped at nothing short of bringing the milkman, bread man and grocer. The part that surprised me the most was not that she wanted the whole world to see the daughter who had predicted her own twins, but that these people would actually accompany her to my house.

Furthermore, they were saying I had ´wished´ my ovaries into releasing two eggs, instead of one. Also that I had subconsciously gone into labor on exactly July 16th. Mind over matter. This annoyed me terribly.

Sharon knew this circus was inevitable. She said if she could somehow struggle into her much-too-tight nurse´s uniform, she´d stand at the door, cap and all, explaining, ´Mommy is resting peacefully -- she´ll call you when she´s in dire need of company´. Sharon unfortunately was in the hospital with a few minor complications, in her last month of pregnancy. Boy, she would have set them straight! Mom was not getting the message. "Zandar´s coming for the weekend. She´s staying with us."

NO, GOD! NO! NOT HER! Just her name could still paralyze me with fright. Being a grown up woman and far beyond her reach did not minimize the terror of seeing this woman. My dear ´great-aunt´, who would stuff food down my throat till I threw up, then belt me for making the mess, was popping in for a friendly visit.

'She can't come here. I won't see her!"

"Donna, how can you say such a thing, after all the help she's been to us? You'll take her to the hospital so she can see my grandchildren," my mother continued, oblivious to the fact that I wanted to forget the horrors of that miserable year -- not entertain them.

Tears automatically streamed down my face as I recalled the Easter Sunday when I was five and a half years old. While Zandar took her afternoon nap, I was free to do as I pleased during those sweet hours. I perched myself on the living room window still, staring, as children do, out to a world I couldn't comprehend. It was a city I didn't recognize, except for the few blocks to my school, a school where no one spoke Croatian, only English.

How long will I be in this dreadful place? I thought back to the nursery school in Austria, recalling more pleasant memories. Here, I wasn't allowed to play. Zandar wouldn't even let me color. "A waste of time," she said.

"MY MOTHER! Zandar, ZANDAR, get up, wake up -- my mother's here -- she's come to get me -- now you'll be sorry -- my mother's here!" Joining me by the window, "Where's your mother?" she yelled angrily.

"Look, see? Way, way over there by those lights. See that taxi -- way over there -- " I pointed, finger pressed to the glass. My ears rang from the blow across my head.

"Stop hitting her!" my uncle was grabbing for her arms. He always tried to stop her, but she still always hit me.

"She woke me up, the brat!" grabbing for me as I backed away.

"She IS coming, she IS! You'll see." I was almost choking, I don't know who was more surprised, her or me when, not more than five minutes later, my mother knocked at the door. She WAS in that taxi.

"Take me home, take me home, NOW! Get me out of here! I HATE her -- she beats me -- she set my hair on fire -- she ties me up, every day, she forces me to write and she squeezes my

37

fingers. I can't WRITE, I can't even print. PLEASE! Take me home." I poured out all the gruelling details as fast as I could manage to talk, without taking a breath. I pleaded with her the entire night and wouldn't let her sleep.

"Your father won't let me. There's no one to watch you. We have to work. Maybe in a month or so."

"I'll be GOOD. I PROMISE! P-L-E-A-S-E! No one has to watch me. Please!"

My mother cried all the way back to Toronto, on the bus, alone, without me.

How can you leave me here? She'll kill me by the time you come back for me. I watched the bus pulling away from the terminal. I'm not going to ever see her again. Zandar's going to kill me.

And now I was expected to entertain this woman? Serve her coffee? Laugh about the good old days? She'd mellowed greatly in her old age, yes, but no, no -- to see her would be to relive a nightmare.

My neck smarted from the stitches. The bandage pulled on the small hairs around my neck. This had been an opportune time to get my cyst removed, before the babies got home, only now I regretted making the decision.

I was just drained, and even more so with the threat of Zandar's visit this weekend. My dad convinced me to wash the kitchen ceiling since all his family were coming for inspection. I had not done much heavy housework while pregnant. Instead of catching up on my rest, to be ship-shape for when the boys came home, I was doing spring cleaning. For what? My friends couldn't care less if my ceiling was clean or dirty. The important thing was to get my dad off my back. Housework somehow seemed easier than arguing with him.

I was in the 'executive office', with a breast pump and wearing only a small towel wrapped around my waist. Every time I would start to pump milk, which would be taken to the hospital for the boys, the phone would ring. Maybe this was the 'million dollar' service call, so I just had to answer that phone. Therefore, I'd assemble all the apparatus and baby bottles on the desk (we had a desk in there now -- a chair too) by the 'executive phone'. If it rang, I could easily take the call without too much disruption.

I heard our front door open. It couldn't be Darko, I'd just hung up with him before I started this procedure. Couldn't be any of my friends, they'd ring the bell.

"Who's there?" I yelled after hearing some commotion, trying desperately to cover a naked body with something not much larger than a face cloth. I heard the sound of doors opening and being closed again, closer and closer, indicating this door was going to open next. "Don't come in here --" Too late. There was my very old, nearly deaf, great-uncle, peering through a five inch opening, hoping he wasn't waking anyone.

Horrors, that someone should see me like this! What would he imagine I was doing? I could see his mind trying to unravel these 'strange' circumstances. This also meant that Zandar was somewhere close behind. I went hysterical. Unless locked in my 'too small' bathroom, I had absolutely no privacy. None. In my own home. Why was it so difficult for Darko to take his key and lock up as he left in the mornings? Why hadn't I checked the door? It was too early, that's why, my MOTHER wouldn't be here for hours yet.

"Gordana," Zandar was surprised! "Why are you so upset?"

"Upset? No. No. I'm not upset. I'll be fine, as soon as everyone either LEAVES or PASSES me some clothes." Shut the door. Get out of here. Who else did they have in the hall?

I'm going to move out into the country some day. Miles from these daily calamities. Somewhere quiet. PRIVATE. Going to get two large dogs. One for each door. -- I can't do that, I'm even terrified of little puppies. But, what about the burglars that prowl these desolate areas? Smarten up -- burglars are okay. They come and quickly slip out before attracting any notice -- it's THE RELATIVES I have to worry about! They appear out of nowhere, PARASITES, devouring, destroying anything which lay in their path.

Finally doctor "D" and Astronaut "M" are ready to come home. Five pounds, eight ounces. Both of them.

The out-law wants to come along when we bring the babies home today. No bloomin´ way lady! You couldn´t come to the hospital for three days to see your grandkids till you´d rested from your trip overseas, you AIN´T gonna intrude, not today. Funny how our ´visitations' and 'appointments´ always have to be compatible with HER personal comfort.

Standing in the nursery, filled with amazement and wonder, finally taking a baby (babies) home from a hospital, I realized I was being torn in two. My heart and soul functioned on two levels; love, warmth, compassion, sensitivity, concern, joy, when I revolved around ´the Prince, Doc and Astronaut´. Hurt, hate, more hurt, resentment, hurt and disgust, when in the presence of all these related ´well wishers´.

My long awaited dreams, now presently being fulfilled, were continually snuffed and quenched by these imposing, break-down-the-door, snoops.

"Donna, you´ve been up for more than twenty-four hours. Get some rest, hon." Darko said with concern in his voice.

"Later, Michael has to eat again in about twenty minutes."

"Why do they have to be fed so often?" This was all new to pops too.

"Their tummies are too small to hold more than a couple of ounces of milk and their weight HAS TO increase as soon as possible." By now, I really sounded like I knew as much as the physicians... even more.

I wished he could feed Danny while I breast fed Michael. That would leave me two hours and fifteen minutes, that no one was feeding, to sleep.

My mind was trying to sort out a schedule. Michael takes forty-five minutes to feed (he was still very slow and difficult to feed from being accustomed to milk being dumped into his stomach). Fifteen minutes later, it was Danny´s turn. Nipples and bottles either ran too fast or no milk seeped through. He'd take another forty-five minutes, at least. Total time consumed feeding them: one hour and forty-five minutes. In thirty minutes I would have to feed Michael, and the whole cycle started again, around the clock, again and again, until they were at least nine pounds. That could take months! I couldn't go months, sleeping only thirty minutes every two hours, much less washing diapers and preparing meals!

PANIC!

I HAVE TO GET SOME HELP. WHERE? WHO? Darko's working sixteen hours a day trying to catch up on the bills. I couldn't afford help even for a couple of hours a day. We were overdrawn more than $1,000 at the bank. Think. Think.

I picked up the phone, dialing relative after relative.

Relative 'A' -- "Sorry, Donna, I have a shower to attend tomorrow, wish I could help."

Relative 'B' -- "Oh no, couldn't sleep over, hubby would never hear of it."

'C' -- "Have to get my hair done tomorrow. Maybe next week."

'D' -- "You'll manage somehow. YOU'RE YOUNG."

I could not believe these lame excuses. "YOU only managed because you had your mother living with you. YOU had your babies one at a time. YOUR babies were full term. YOURS didn't need to eat every two hours. YOURS could suck properly." I screamed and pleaded in desperation.

My panic intensified. Three days later, I had gone four without sleep and was too overwrought to eat in all this time. I tried again, but X, Y, and Z all had the same excuses. I was stunned. They were the same people whose income tax forms, unemployment forms, compensation and old age forms I had filled out for all these years. I'd registered their kids in school, accompanied or driven them to get marriage licenses, driver's licenses, passports, and visa's. Guaranteed jobs for THEIR friends and their relatives whom we had never even met. I had been a social service, an information center, a chauffeur and a non-profit organization for years to these 'folks'. It was expected. It was owed. We were family. Then! Now I'm talking life and death; mine; and they have to get their HAIR DONE!

Day five: "Dana, where do you keep the salt? ... Dana, don't you have any shortening? ... Dana, I can't find a large enough pot... I'll never be able to cook Darko a good meal in this place."

"PLEASE, don't wake me up unless it's feeding time. I HAVE TO SLEEP TILL THEN."

In-law, out-law, whatever she was, just continued: "Who dirtied all these dishes? It'll take me all night to clean this mess."

"Never mind the dishes. I'll do them NEXT MONTH. MYSELF."

I tried to eat but my stomach had shrunk so much it rejected food and I would chuck it up.

Day six, 5:00 a.m.: I had not needed or even thought of food. Must eat something. I feel weak. What if I drop one of the babies? I'm so dizzy. So weak. Then I remembered Sara. Sara! She'll come. I just know it.

"Sara? Remember? We met a few weeks ago. I'm the one with the twins. This is an emergency. Please come over, right now. It's their feeding time and I'm too weak to pick them up."

She arrived within minutes, in her nightgown and housecoat. Took complete charge of both boys. Fed, powdered, changed, made new formula. I now had NO milk, for either one.

I watched here efficiency. I was like that, just a few weeks ago. What happened? Why am I IMMOBILIZED? I see what she's doing. I CAN do what she's doing. But I'M not. WHY NOT? What am I going to do when she leaves? What about tomorrow?

"Couldn't your mother help, dear?" She was so-o-o concerned.

"She says she's afraid of them, never having been near a baby. That's why my grandmother took care of me. She's afraid she'll drop one. There's no way, after a proclamation like that, that I could sleep while she fed them."

"What about a girlfriend?"

"I couldn't impose on my girlfriends for help. They have small babies and young families of their own. Most are experiencing similar turmoil. I expected family to help. I expected it without even having to ask for it. I haven't asked anyone, anything, till now. The rest of my highschool friends have moved far away. Darko's sister is in Vancouver. There's NOBODY!"

I woke up in a hospital. I had passed out while Sara was there. The doctor was saying, "Exhaustion. Sheer and simple exhaustion. You'll be fine in a day or two. You just need some nourishment and a couple of nights' sleep."

"I can't cope."

"Of course you can't. Who expects you to? Get some help."

"Easier said than done, doctor. I've got a little problem in that department."

Six days after I was admitted, I was back home. STRONG. DETERMINED. CHANGED.

A Red Cross homemaker arrived. She came not only to help me cope and let me sleep through an occasional night, but to also get it through my head, for my own good and the good of the babies, to be forceful and put my foot down when people showed up at 11:30 at night or 8:00 in the morning to socialize. She had never in her life seen so many people. "I don't care who they are. Throw them out. If they're not here to wash diapers ... Slam the door."

Good idea. Finally I had someone actually backing ME.

"Sorry, I don't want company." PERIOD. "No you can't see the twins. Come back in six years, I'll let you register them in school, like I did your son."

"How am I doing? How are the boys? -- Just fine. Why don't you come over when they're old enough to learn how to drive. I'll let you teach them, like I taught you. Remember?"

"Oh, so you think I should have a christening party for at least 70, maybe 80. GOT TO HELL! Don't show up at my door, ever again."

"What's wrong, Donna? What's happened, Donna? Why are you angry, Donna?"

"Angry? Me? No. No. I'll be fine, just as long as you stay out of my life. Call ONLY if you need your fuses changed or your rec room wired, BUT ONLY IF YOU'RE PLANNING TO PAY next time. We're not family A-N-Y-M-O-R-E!":

"Cica, our pet name for Darko's sister Maria, had arrived back from B.C. She was just three months younger than me. A real knockout. Long, blond naturally curly hair. Blue eyed, petite, tiny thing (if you can imagine anyone closely related to 'humungous Darko being described by the adjective 'PETITE'). She could really stop traffic, and I don't mean with muscle, like her brother.

She was crying. "Why didn't you notify me? I would have come, immediately. In an instant. You know I WOULD."

I knew she meant it from the bottom of her heart. Maria had never had a problem telling people what was on her mind, and she couldn't care less what people thought of HER. She wouldn't offer help unless she could give her 'all'.

She loved the boys, and was thrilled at becoming an aunt.

"I can't imagine ME being anyone's aunt." she laughed. "It sounds so matronly."

She was only 22, yet sadly bitter, knowing life had somehow short-changed her. Now she wanted it all at once.

"Donna, I'm not ever going to have kids. I could never contemplate having kids. Who needs the hassle? I have too much living to catch up on."

Over the next few years she traveled the world. Worked her way from one corner of the globe to the other. We hardly saw one another. When we did, we were the sister that each had longed for while growing up. We were complete opposites, with the exception of our mutual gift for gab. A year's worth of catching up could be accomplished in one evening. Next year, we'd continue, same time, same place, like there'd never been an interval.

"Hello, police department. Have there been any reports of wolves in this neighborhood?"

"Wolves, Ma'am? Well, there is always a possibility."

"I'm certain that there's a pack of three, in my backyard, tearing apart someone's chicken."

Well now, the wolves didn't get too big a response but ---

"A chicken? A dead one? What's a chicken doing in your back yard?"

"It's dead now, officer. Everyone around here has chickens, pigeons, you name it. Right in the middle of this suburb."

"We'll send someone right over."

Now "I" was watching from behind the curtains. In minutes, two cruisers pulled up, and two officers, guns drawn, cautiously entered through my gate. The first one walked over to one of these 'wolves', tilted his cap high on his head, as his eyes searched for the window I was positioned at. Now I've done it. I answered the door, embarrassed and blushing down to my toes. "They looked like wolves to me."

"Ma'am, are you by any chance frightened of German Shepherds?"

"Did you see the chicken? They tore it apart." I exclaimed.

"Yes. Now that´s a different story. Something that you should definitely be concerned about. They WILL attract wild animals. We´ll make a report. Find out who´s keeping them and how many. Have a good day."

"Sharon, we have to get away from this neighborhood."

"The only way I could get hubby to move is if his entire family would agree. Oh-h-h! I have an idea! You´re really going to love this one."

"What?" She really had me curious.

"Still got your OUIJA board?"

"Yeah."

"Well, if I were to speak strictly Portuguese during a séance, and everyone knows YOU don´t speak a word of PORTUGUESE, dumb Canadian that you are, and if ´OUIJA´ answered all my questions correctly, it would have to be a spirit, right?"

"I LOVE IT! HOW?"

"Easy. We´ll practice, I´ll teach you the key words, such as ´move´, ´house´, and so on. If I say ´Oh, Ouija´, the answer will be ´yes´. If I only say ´Ouija´, then the answer will be ´no´."

Needless to say, we scared them out of their skins. But, yes, Sharon would be moving too. With their blessings! ***

***Just in case even one person puts down this book and runs out to buy a Ouija board and have some fun, before reading part two of this book: WARNING -- THIS IS NOT A GAME. IT IS NOT A TOY. IT IS DANGEROUS BUSINESS. YOU WOULD BE DABBLING WITH THE OCCULT. I will discuss this topic further in part two.

We quickly developed the hang of having some real fun, bored housewives that we´d become. Another brain storm over coffee one day. The caffeine was to blame for this one; we were definitely over-stimulated when we came up with it. We needed something to keep our minds and spirits alert. We´d start our own business.

"What, telling fortunes?"

"No, they´d catch on too quickly if we did it too often. A store maybe. YES! A boutique. Everyone´s into GO-GO watches and mini´s and maxi´s."

"You think we could talk the guys into giving us some money to start?"

"Sure, it´ll keep us out of their hair and we don´t need much anyway."

We were both surrounded by relatives who negated our every move. We needed an identity of our own. This just might be it.

All the work and typing and bookkeeping for Darko´s business kept me busy. But that was all WORK. This was going to be FUN. Our only prerequisite was that the store had to be large enough for three playpens.

Since Sharon was born on November 3rd and I on November 6th, we naturally named our boutique "Scorpio". We hit the front page of the local papers, with a half page article and a picture of me modeling a black lace, see-through, mini dress. I was dreadfully shy and the photographer had to do a lot of ´hide all the peek-a-boo´s.

The babies were on the floor at my feet. The Newspaper piece read as follows:

SCORPIO OPENS

A mother of six month old twin boys who opens a mod boutique has to be a superwoman.

That´s Donna Martonfi, who is selling mini dresses and plastic chairs while twins, Daniel and Michael, play in the back room.

Mrs. Martonfi, and co-partner, Mrs. Sharon ......, a housewife and mother of a five month old daughter, are operating Scorpio on Lakeshore Road.

Neither had previous experience in business when they decided to open a shop while drinking coffee one day.

"Our husbands probably think we're crazy, but they helped us finance it," said Sharon.

The girls christened it 'Scorpio' because that is their zodiac sign.

The gear sold in the shop, formerly Fowler's Real Estate, includes peek-a-boo umbrellas and raincoats, wet-look skirts, inflatable chairs (in future); maxi coats, slacks and imitation snakeskin coats, from Mr. D.

The Scorpians want to provide inexpensive popular clothes for office girls and teenagers."

Sharon could not be talked into having her picture taken. She had even a lower self-image than I did. "I'm two feet taller than all my relatives."

"Sharon, your relatives are Portuguese. Exceptionally short ones at that."

"No way. Beside the babies I'll look ten feet tall, whether in a mini or a maxi."

Needless to say, it was a disaster. When all the rug crawlers in the playpens became mountain climbers, our dresses had to be suspended from wagon wheels which were attached to the ceiling. The spokes substituted for racks. With three babies, it was no use. I gave up long before Sharon. At least I had the latest wardrobe, and when we parted in business, boxes of belts, jewelry and dresses were stored away as my share of the investment.

Months passed, and I was really catching on. Raising babies was all I had hoped it would be, and even more. Not only were we happy and healthy, we prospered to the point that the $1,000 overdraft was allowed to climb to $3,000, no questions asked.

"Darko, I'd save a lot of time if I had a washer and dryer and didn't have to run to the laundromat. You think you could swing a set?"

I should have stressed the part about 'one set'. The same day, I ended up with my own laundromat! Darko pulled up in a moving van.

"Donna, I bought forty-three washers and dryers!"

"Forty-three?"

"No eighty-six in total."

"I don't have that many diapers. ARE YOU KIDDING?"

"No, Listen, NONE of them work. I'll repair them. You put an ad in the paper. We'll sell them from the basement. We'll be able to pay off the overdraft in no time.

Some months later, after purchasing a carpet, I should have known better than to ask for a vacuum cleaner. NINETY! Yes sir . . . instantly, I was in the vacuum cleaner business. Never, NEVER will I ask for another appliance. My $15.00 refrigerator will just have to go to the grave with me. When the kids get old enough to walk I'll never be able to find them in this mess.

Since we had a 'mess' of washers, dryers, vacuums, belts, buckles, you name it, we decided we would try our luck at a flea market. Get rid of some of this junk, especially since we were going to move. Maybe we could move our inventory a bit quicker, in greater volumes, than one by one through ads.

It was only early September but a dreadful, bone-chilling day. I was really getting cold. "Darko, I'm freezing. Let's go."

"We're just starting to sell. How can you be COLD? Put on my jacket."

It didn't help. A vendor nearby noticed that my lips had turned blue and brought the sheep skins he was selling to bundle me up. It was too late. I couldn't stop shaking. Nobody else was cold. Just me. Darko took me home and I climbed into bed telling him to look after the boys for the rest of the day and send the baby-sitter home.

I had hot and cold chills. A fever so high I was perspiring, yet shaking, from cold. Darko made some hot tea with honey and wrapped me in a thick quilt, tied around my waist so I couldn't uncover myself overnight. He didn't know I put the boys in a cool tub when they had a fever. I was in no shape to realize anything. All night he called doctor after doctor from the phone book. Nobody made house calls anymore. "Take her to a hospital," they replied, "if she's that bad." By the time he reached the 'F's' he located a sweet doc who came within minutes.

"She has pneumonia. Her fever's so high we'll have to take her to the hospital. You should have kept her cool."

"She was freezing, I didn't want her to catch pneumonia. We've got nobody to look after the babies. She'll never stay in the hospital unless she can bring them along."

"Okay, fine. I'll leave her till morning. If there's no improvement she'll have to go in."

Darko had left in the morning to do a quick emergency call. He had put the playpen and the kids by my bed after feeding and changing them, and told them not to move. "Stay there and watch TV until I get back. Don't wake mommy. She's sick."

When I woke up I had big red spots all over my body. 'The fever's made me delirious', I thought.

Just then Darko walked in. "WHAT ARE THOSE SPOTS?" He ran to the bed.

"Do you see them too?"

This sweet doc was always there when you needed him. "Don't panic. I'll be right over."

He took one look at me and said, "She's allergic to penicillin and STOP SMOKING."

I couldn't even sit up, but I COULD smoke. I quit until 5:00 p.m. but didn't feel any better. I couldn't feel any worse, s-o-o-o since I slept for most of the night and day, the few I snuck couldn't hurt.

My mother had faced the humiliation of not being around when I needed her the last time and now had talked my dad into letting her come every day. She sat on the corner of my bed crying, sobbing and howling.

"What are you going to do? Who's going to bring them up? You're going to die. I told you to eat more. You and your stupid diets. See what's happened. Why are you still smoking?"

I had to use a bed pan because I had become too weak to go as far as the bathroom. I would bend over and change one diaper and then have to lay back, heaving and gasping for air, before I could change the other. She was sitting far away so that I couldn't get at her, ten hours a day, just crying.

"Why don't you change a diaper?" I had to take three breaths between each word. "Either help or get out!"

My dad had phoned dozens of times, upset over the fact that she wasn't at the store, helping. He couldn't close the store to take his afternoon nap (he couldn't make it through the day without one).

"What is she doing over there? How much cleaning is there?" he yelled.

"She's NOT scrubbing pots and washing diapers! She's NOT helping. I can't even get her to get a baby bottle from the fridge, which I DO need. Don't let her come. I don't want her here. Keep her home. She's driving me crazy sitting on the edge of my bed crying all day."

I was throwing things at her. Pillows, diapers, anything I could reach to get her out of my room. The boys thought it was a game. I had a whole day's supply of diapers, water, juice, anything I might need. Anything that wouldn't damage a wall or break a mirror, I threw at her. She hid behind the door and continued, "What's going to happen to those poor children when you die?"

"Mother, you're going to die as soon as I'm strong enough to get out of bed. GET OUT OF HERE!"

I was determined I was going to get better quickly, just so I could strangle her. She'd always leave before Darko got home. He would phone my dad and insist that he not allow her to come again.

Next morning I picked up the phone and called the hospitals, the police station and the fire department, explaining if someone didn't come to get her, I would get worse, not better.

"Ma'am, unless she's a physical threat to the life of you or herself, there is nothing we can do."

"But if I could reach her, I would kill her."

"Sorry, Ma'am. We can't help you."

Now, realizing that I was serious, she was threatening to throw herself under the next train that went by.

"Good, do it! Just get out and don't come back."

My guilt was unbearable. She wouldn't do it. She was too much of a Catholic. I felt like a monster, but I had to think of myself first. I had to. I had enough to cope with, without dealing with her.

Why did I feel so guilty? She left me to die on top of the Alps. My uncle told me, many times, if it hadn't been for him, I would still be three and a half years old, frozen to death on top of a mountain. I was too heavy for her to carry. My uncle then took me and put me in a nap sack on his back and carried me into Austria. She left me again, with Zandar. Why do I feel as if I owe her, to feel sorry for her? Why?

Who cares? I have to get better.

Having the boys right in my room, beside me all day, they quickly learned how to say many words. They'd point at the TV and say 'GOOK', meaning look; 'WALU', meaning water. In the five weeks it took me to recuperate, they really grew, in more ways than one. Talking to them, singing songs, teaching them games; I enjoyed every minute.

Nancy, a girl that was one of my regular sitters, showed up at the door one morning. "Donna, could you drive me to work?"

"I'm sorry, I've got pneumonia."

"You just have to drive me." she persisted. "I have to go to work."

"I can't, I'm too sick. Take a taxi.'

"I can't afford a taxi. You just have to drive me."

"Don't you understand?" I was absolutely furious! "I'm sick! Besides, I don't work. I have to support a car, the license plates, the insurance and the upkeep, so I can drive everyone on the block wherever they have to go. I have become everyone's taxi, taking them to jobs where they are earning wages! You can't afford a taxi but I suppose I can afford to be everyone's free taxi." I slammed the door. People still took me for a doormat.

The next day I had a ruder awakening. I walked the few doors to Shirley's house, to retrieve my iron which I had loaned her five weeks before. Instead of answering her door, she came to the second floor balcony and bluntly exclaimed, "You can't have it back today, I have to iron Mark's pants."

"Shirley, I have to go to the doctor's and I have to iron my pant suit."

"Mark'll be furious if his pants aren't ironed."

"I don't care Shirley, you've had it five weeks."

"I'll bring it to you tomorrow."

I couldn't believe the gall of her. "It's my damn iron, bring it to me NOW!" I had to beg to get my own iron back! Wasn't anyone normal?

By the time I got to the doctor's office I thought my blood pressure would be through the roof. The doctor couldn't believe my X-rays. "The way you smoke Donna, and pneumonia as well,

I really expected the worst. But your lungs are as healthy as a newborn´s."

He shouldn´t have told me that, not if he ever wanted to see me quit smoking. At least I found a flaw in this man; otherwise he´d be a perfect human being.

Chapter Five

ANOTHER MIRACLE? -- SOUNDS MORE LIKE A MISTAKE

We finally got an offer on our semi. "You're getting $1,000 more than you've asked for, just to move out in ten days, what's the problem?" asked the agent.

"Find a house and move in only ten days? No problem. SEE YA — BYE!"

There aren't many districts you can go house hunting that allow panel trucks, ladders, washers, dryers, vacuums, and so on to be piled in the driveway, but this time we had a 'good' agent.

"It'll have to be a fairly busy street and I have just the one."

The home had everything we wanted. A fireplace in the living room, another fireplace in a finished rec room with wall to wall shelves for Darko's books. It was a few thousand costlier than we had anticipated, but never-the-less, detached; no chickens, no pigeons; only traffic and noise.

You have to visualize this location. To our north was a hydro field, and privacy. To the south, our one and only neighbour. So our house started a stretch of only nine homes on this section of the street. No one across from us and no one, just a field, beside us. Did I say no chickens or pigeons? This was not a slum district, either. Our one and only neighbour had a running total of thirty-four cats.

Now these were not ordinary cats. The majority of them were cross-bred stock, many dragging their hind legs behind them. The 'healthier' toms were allowed to prowl at night on busy traffic-congested streets and were coming back with amputated tails, ears and missing eyes. They were grotesque — stitched up, everywhere.

We were ready to celebrate, after the movers left, with a box of cream squares. This was a delicacy, because Darko and I were always dieting. Minutes after I had set the table, I found one of these 'monsters' on top of our kitchen table, devouring our feast.

Aluminum doors were ordered the same day. Next, they were intruding through the basement windows, so naturally we had to install air conditioning.

To a family that had just stretched a few thousand beyond their limit, this added expense alone should have been the straw that broke the camel's back.

Not yet. We only owed about $35,000.00.

I don't want to stir up any animosity among animal lovers, but Darko HATED cats and dogs at this point. (A year after we moved in, the lady next door was found dead in her bed. The autopsy showed she died from a hair ball stuck in her esophagus). Her husband took over a dozen kittens, put them in a plastic garbage bag, laid them on the driveway and drove his car back and forth across the bag. He bragged to the kids how easy it was to get rid of them. The rest he locked out of the house, and he wouldn't feed them.

They roamed the streets for months afterwards. Darko always had a thing about animal hair getting stuck in his throat. Whenever he visited friends that had a cat or dog, a hair would inevitably end up in his mouth. He would no more have a cat or dog in the house than he would a pig or goat, but even he thought this man was a revolting, inhumane ogre.

A new home means a new baby, or some such folk tale so Darko wasn't taking any chances. "Donna, I was thinking about all the fortune tellers you've been to that said we were going to have three boys and a girl. I didn't plan on ever having four children. This is getting too close for comfort. Are you taking your pill?"

"Faithfully, Honey."

"I don't want to take any chances. Two sons to put through school is plenty. Especially for the careers they're going to have."

"You gave me an idea. I have a plan. I've always wanted the excess skin on my stomach removed, until I heard how much it was going to cost. If I had my tubes tied at the same time, it would cost peanuts. Our medical plan would cover it." Why hadn't I thought of this before?

Prepared, and always ready for all action, I quickly got on the buzzer. The doctor (I wouldn't let Dr. Moore know I didn't want more babies, she could be Catholic) came well recommended. "You're scheduled for June the first. Take your pill, regardless, till then. If at any time, ANY TIME AT ALL, you should change your mind — change it freely. I don't approve of tubal ligation, especially when you're not even twenty-four years old. You have a long life ahead."

Change my mind? Are you kidding? I would have to run around with this juggly pot forever. This is my chance. Bikinis were in style.

1:00 p.m. June 1, 1972

"Mrs. Martonfi", the voice over the phone sounded surprised, "you've been scheduled to check in by noon. Are you coming?"

My voice, a whisper, "No, no. I've changed my mind." Whose voice is that? It can't be mine. I've been looking forward to this for three years.

Darko was even more surprised to find me home. "Chicken out?"

"No, not chicken—I can't really explain it. I've changed my mind."

"That does it. Now I'm certain, Donna, it's too close for comfort; three boys, one girl. I'm having a vasectomy. Anyway, your stomach doesn't need fixing, it's a beautiful souvenir — not just anyone has TWINS. It'll be your special identification mark."

"That's sweet — yes — but — still — YUK. What more proof do I need than them?" I asked, pointing at the boys. "I'm a beautiful witch, with a lovely, shrivelled stomach. What next?"

How we laughed when we heard the vasectomy was scheduled right on Darko's birthday. It wasn't the really "IN" thing to do as of yet.

Baka Sisa (I had rechristened my out-law. Baka meaning grandma; Sisa, our pet name for Darko's sister, Maria. Motherhood must have mellowed me slightly) demanded of Darko: "How can you let her talk you into giving up your manhood? On your birthday, yet! I won't hear of it."

Well, shut your ears then, lady, I thought. Better yet, unstop your ears; shut your mouth. "It's your son that doesn't want any more children, it's not my idea."

She shot me a glare. "I knew you could talk him into anything. BUT THIS?"

"HAPPY BIRTHDAY, DEAR DARKO!!! ..."

Somewhere, about two months later, near the end of August, Darko noticed something v-e-r-y unusual. "You're finally getting top heavy. Those exercises really work."

"I'm a little concerned, Darko. I don't do them anymore."

"Go get examined then. You never can be certain about breast cancer."

"I don't think they'd GROW, you know, if it was breast cancer." My mind flashed a thought. It just couldn't be. The only other time my breasts enlarged...

"I should say there's a reason you're engorged, Mrs. Martonfi," Dr. Ried chuckled. "You're roughly four months pregnant. I told you to take your pill right up to and for a week after the vasectomy."

"But I did. I DID. The operation wasn't even two months ago."

"People have been known to get pregnant on the pill. CONGRATULATIONS."

The idea grew on me quickly. Just as long as it isn't TWO again this time, God. Don't send two, okay?

How do I nicely explain to Darko that the fortune tellers were right? I've got a strong feeling this is going to be a boy.

"Darko, Honey, SURPRISE! We've caused some rumors among our relatives in our day, ha, ha. What do you think they're going to say now, ha, ha?"

We were almost doubled over with laughter knowing we'd put his mother into complete shock. I want to be there when she tries to calculate from June 29th, the day her son was ´castrated´, (she could never get that straight) till February 24th, 1973. Less than eight months, tootsie. Not even eight months. Was it feminine intuition? Instinct? I was already carrying a tiny life, on June 1st.

Did I say shock? I went into shock.

"What did she just say" Dr. Ried asked, more than surprised behind the surgical mask.

"She said something about her baby being ugly," one of the nurses replied.

"Oh, no, God, I didn't mean ugly!" I didn't, it's just—-You have to understand, I've had three, blue eyed, blond (peach fuzz) babies. He just couldn't look like this! You would have to see this little monkey. He had pitch black hair, down past his eyes, side burns that almost connected over his upper lip to form a mustache, bruises from the forceps at the side of his temples and black tiny hairs that ran down his spine, to his waist, AND... protruding at the centre of all this black hair, was a gigantic nose.

WAS THIS GUY EVER GOING TO START TONGUES WAGGING!

Not only was he hairy; the water at the hospital was shut down for a few hours at the time of his birth, so he never was properly cleaned. He was a mess. I tried to hide him under his blanket when the nurses brought him, while looking over at the 'peach-fuzz' blondie brought to the girl in the next bed. I expected that baby. He looked more like mine than this one.

I seriously wondered how I was going to explain him to relatives, such as to the one who wanted to know what happened to the astronauts on the moon IN THE DAY TIME. 'Oh, they just go poof.'

The third day after his arrival, I reached out my arms to take my amusing bundle from the nurse and fell in love with the most beautiful child God ever created. I thought they had handed me the wrong one. All the facial hair had fallen off. The jet-black hair was curled, in one of those funny little rolls. All clean and shiny and scrubbed. And... his nose wasn't big at all.

Not at all. Overwhelming love flooded through me.

"Don't you worry little fellow. You've just made it into the world by the skin of your teeth. God must have a special plan or you." Not only that, for some reason, this pregnancy had corrected the loose, overstretched skin from the twins. It looked 200% better now.

My dad stood at the nursery window, tears streaming down his face. (I still couldn't get used to my tall, handsome dad, crying. It just didn't seem like him. WE, well — we just never cried. Only mother cried — not us).

"He looks just like you, when you were born. I can see you now, like it was just yesterday. When the nurse brought you and showed me my daughter." Actually I thought little Stevie looked just like him.

I wish I could say the relatives had learned the first time around I wasn't going to be a cream puff or a door mat to wipe their feet on anytime they fancied. They hadn't. Now they were pushing their luck.

"How can you do such a thing to Darko?"

"Do such a thing to Darko???" I acted surprised. "Why, I don't know what you mean."

"It's more than obvious to us, about this kid."

"Really? Oh, you've got it all wrong — this one's Darko's -- it's the other three that aren't. Why don't you go read a book. As a matter of fact go read a couple of hundred. Come back in half a century when you've learned something. And oh, by the way, GET OUT OF MY HOUSE."

This time I was in TOP shape. Steven was a gift sent from God. HE wanted me to know how easy it was to have just one baby. The bottle of milk was slurped before I could get comfortable in my easy chair (still didn't get that rocker. I was afraid to ask. I didn't want to end up with a furniture store). Then, to our astonishment, he'd sleep for four hours. We'd stand over him waiting for him to wake up. That child just NEVER cried. We worried that he didn't know how. As soon as his eyes opened, he'd shove his fist into his mouth and suck with all his might until I'd replace his fist with a bottle of milk. Not a peep out of him. Then, back to sleep for another four hours. Unbelievable, I had TIME to enjoy Stevie.

I'm ashamed to admit he was such a quite, undemanding baby that one day, mommy, daddy, doc and astro were pulling out of the driveway when Darko and I simultaneously shot each other a ghastly look, both realizing at the same moment we had literally forgotten to take him with us to the car.

Usually there was a huge commotion when all four of us were leaving together. By the time I'd have the second twin dressed — hat, gloves, boots, mitts and shawl — the first, so bundled only his eyes showed, would have to go to the bathroom. Then vice-versa. It took an hour to get from the front hall to the car. BUT TO ACTUALLY FORGET HIM! I hope he never hears this story.

Continuing happily along. . . I decided that housewife, mother, cook, nursemaid, dishwasher (no — wouldn't ask for a dishwasher either) bookkeeper, typist, general manager (of a hardly-manageable electrical business) and appliance salesman, was just not enough. I needed more — a job. A job that pays. "What job?", I wondered.

Coincidentally, a good high school friend, Jan, who worked for the Provincial Courts, advised that their Croatian/Serbian/Yugoslavian (same as English/American/Canadian) interpreter was ready to retire. Would I want to take her place on a freelance basis?

You bettcha! With the money I'd make I could get a live-in babysitter and untie my apron strings, just enough. It was only a few mornings or days a week. I would then not have to pay a sitter on Friday and Wednesday nights, our special nights to go out and get away from all the phone calls and numerous businesses. She could watch the kids while I did Darko's typing and bookkeeping, at a more reasonable and decent hour than midnight. I went through eleven girls in eighteen months. I COULD write a whole book on these 'sitters'. Maybe another time. I'll just briefly outline the reasons why they did not work out, before I continue with my story:

They had their own apartment in the basement, with full use of the rec room. I only went downstairs to do the laundry. They had a TV in their room, a private bath and air conditioning. All the conveniences that they did not have to earn for themselves. It was as luxurious as living in a hotel, and getting paid to boot. Not bad for just watching three kids, making grilled cheese sandwiches for lunch and washing dishes.

Most references that I called said roughly the same thing. "Don't ask her to vacuum, she nicks the furniture. Don't ask her to wash clothes unless you want everything dyed red. Also, don't let her dust, she's dropped many irreplaceable wedding gifts. It's impossible to get decent help." I thought I was going to be the exception, because all I wanted was a babysitter with dishwashing services, five days a week. Not much to ask. I went from paying $15.00 per week, to as much as $75.00.

SITTER #1 After she moved in, she said she was a witch, the seventh daughter of a seventh daughter. If we didn't treat her real nice she was going to put a spell on all of us. "Thanks but, no thanks! You can start packing your bags tonight!"

SITTER #2 This one stole $20.00 a week from my purse for three weeks before I could catch her and prove it. $20.00, in my situation, was more than noticeable, especially when it would disappear between the time I got home from the bank on a Friday night until I went to do the shopping on Saturday.

SITTER #3 She wanted $75.00 per week because she worked for an agency and would do all my housework. My sheets sparkled, but she never paid any attention to the kids. She was too busy, so I ended up typing at midnight once again. She insisted on keeping her apartment in the city and returning home each and every weekend. This meant leaving Friday afternoon by 4:30 and then returning Monday, always two to three hours late because she missed her bus, making ME late for work. During the week I would have to drive her to doctor's appointments, Bible study and her weekly hairdresser appointments. Sorry, much too costly, in time AND money.

SITTER #4 A seemingly sweet, elderly lady who was Jehovah's Witness. She hadn't worked for a couple of years but did give references from her previous employer, a Toronto lawyer who had teen-age kids. She hated clutter and emptied all our drawers and cupboards. It looked as if we had moved out. No scissors, no scotch tape, no knick-knacks, no pictures, nothing. Everything was put in boxes and taken to the basement. She studied her Bible every night at 9 o'clock and would not allow me to do Darko's typing as it disturbed her concentration. Many times she came upstairs and asked us to shut our TV off, NOT DOWN BUT OFF, because she needed her beauty sleep. She demanded to be allowed to spank the kids as it was the only way to discipline children. I took a harsh stand on that and said she would be dismissed if she ever hit the kids. I caught her slapping Stevie, on three separate occasions, the last being when he rolled a ball across the top of the pool table.

"You will not hit my children, under any circumstance much less for such trivial reasons. They do not misbehave; and when they do, all you have to do is tell me. Do you understand?"

One evening, Darko and I were on our way out as she mentioned that her ex-husband would be stopping by for a visit. He was on his way to the west coast from the east. She ran off with him that same evening, leaving a note and three children unattended, by themselves. The twins were old enough to call their grandfather and tell him what happened. Coming home around midnight, I panicked when I saw my father's car in our driveway.

I called the police to charge her with desertion and was told that "parents are solely responsible for their children and cannot charge anyone else that they pay to care for them." The only and best thing to do was call the lawyer whom she had given as a reference and advise him that she would again probably give his name and to warn the next family, through him.

SITTER #5 A twenty-three year old Hungarian girl who was hyperactive, and would get more than hysterical if Stevie didn't finish his lunch. Her relatives advised her she could demand all 3-day long weekends off, with pay. "What do you think this is, a union outfit?"

SITTER #6 A seventeen year old girl who climbed out the bathroom window in the middle of the first night, because she was told she would have to learn how to make sandwiches or macaroni and cheese for the kids for lunch. We found the door locked, a chair propped on top of the toilet seat, and saw the prints in the snow outside the basement window. I was a couple of hours late for work.

SITTER #7 When I went to do the wash, a few days after she moved in, I nearly jumped out of my skin when a 6 foot 3 inch black man, in his underwear, ran from the rec room to her bedroom. She failed to ask if her cousin (cousin -- my foot) could live with her. If he couldn't stay (and I pay them to live there) then neither would she.

SITTER #8 Every day, for two weeks, I would come home to find her sound asleep, outside under a tree, the kids inside by themselves. She didn't get severance pay either.

SITTER #9 Her finance came over every evening. He didn't like the rec room. We would find him sleeping on our living room sofa (probably expecting Darko and I to sit on the floor).

He'd sit up, only after much prodding, and ask when I would have supper ready. He could put away more than all six of us. I couldn't afford her, her finance, or our grocery bill.

SITTER #10 Finally, after one year of searching, I found the one I'd always hoped for. She was a school teacher from Trinidad. The kids loved her. She did housekeeping without being asked to. She was courteous, intelligent, sweet, and she wanted to be a part of the family. I was heartbroken months later when she advised that she would be leaving for a higher paying job so she could save enough money to get married and sponsor her finance to Canada. She had been taking correspondence courses and had finally graduated. I knew I could never replace her. She was one of a kind. "My cousin is very much like me. A hard worker and good with kids. She's a Christian too. Why don't you sponsor her to Canada? I'll wait till she arrives."

SITTER #11 (Number 10's cousin) Time was of the essence. I went through the proper channels, but there was a long postal strike in Canada. I wired her a ticket and later waited for her papers to arrive, which got stuck in the mail. I left for the airport at 6:30 p.m., in a raging snow blizzard. She was detained by immigration and I was under "some sort of detainment" (probably arrest) as I was not even allowed to make a phone call to my husband to advise him that I hadn't had an accident. By 4:00 a.m. I realized I was under suspicion for trying to get an alien into Canada illegally. I had also spelled her last name without an 'E' which caused the authorities to suspect I was trying to pull something over on them. Who would think of spelling 'Ford' with an 'E'?

Really becoming upset, I asked to be either officially arrested or to be immediately released. I was released on the promise I would appear at an immigration hearing at 9:00 a.m., sharp, in less than five hours.

The hearing obviously did not go well. The immigration officer's report was so misleading that I wet myself from fright, imagining I would have to go to jail.

She was deported, the same day.

NO MORE LIVE-IN SITTERS! I decided that I would have to find a neighbour I could take the kids to.

(Now, permit me to continue where I left off, before describing these various sitters)

My dad had mentioned so many times how I shouldn't grin so much. Those ugly little teeth made my nose look even larger. Now with my mad money that I was going to make, I could get them all pulled and replaced with 'Hollywood' teeth.

With a part-time job, new teeth and looking forward to my first live-in baby-sitter, I was certain life's problems were really beginning to get sorted out. I knew nobody could figure out why they were treading on thin ice if they mentioned either my teeth, nose, small chest, weight or stomach; but those things really hurt.

I solved the weight and I solved the overstretched stomach problems. I'm till working on the chest (those bust developers really work). Now, finally, out came the teeth.

"Donna, you look great. What did you do, get a nose job?"

"No, I didn't have my nose fixed, I got my teeth out and my nose shrunk, HONEST. If I had a nose job, do you think I'd pick one like this?"

My self-image started to improve but being self-conscious took years longer to rectify.

The night before I was to tackle my new career as an interpreter, I had visions of myself standing in the witness box, my gums still swollen, babbling away, and then suddenly, my teeth jetting straight out of my mouth and landing on the floor at the feet of the crown attorney. Horrors.

They did look great. I hoped I'd never regret this irreversible decision.

Not only had I not made a mistake, I could now grin right around my head till I was silly and no one would tell me to close my mouth. I developed a confidence I never had before. Now when family made comments such as; "How can you have such long nails, don't you do any housework?" or "You're a mother now, you should not be running around with hair down to your waist." or "Don't you think you should start looking like a wife and mother?" I could actually come back with, "If you don't like it, you can lump it. You don't think I would actually want to look like you, do you? Not for all the tea in China."

I was becoming my own person and I didn't care who didn't approve. I could finally hold my own. I didn't have to take ridicule or insults from anyone. "I kinda like the new ME and I ain't gonna change for YOU."

Obviously, when I'd tasted the thrill of having some spending money, a few mornings a week in court just was not going to be enough. I needed a real job. Wonder where I could find a secretarial job which would allow me time off for translating? Guess what? --- I found one!

Knowing I was a worker and a doer, I answered an ad which read:

"SENIOR, EXECUTIVE, CONFIDENTIAL SECRETARY TO THE PRESIDENT" — HOURS: 10:00 TO 3:00

Imagine. Could I? Should I? I was good, but I couldn't spell without the aid of a dictionary. By the time they find out I can't spell, they'll see what a WHIZ I am and keep me anyway. How do I persuade them I need extra time, from these short hours, for court?

Easy . . . The President, as it turned out, was so blown away by my sheer nerve, I was hired on the spot. He constantly travelled and agreed that I could have the most flexible hours in the history of secretarial work. As long as I put in twenty-five hours per week, he didn't care if I did his reports at midnight, at home, or on Saturdays.

The paycheque definitely matched the title, and I became uncomfortable at how little I did for the money I was earning. The boss, Mr. 'H', ranted about how I was his right arm. I was used to doing so much more work for Darko's business that I didn't feel that I was doing anything. The president would travel for weeks on end and there I would sit, in my own office, reading pocket books. I did, however, need the five hour rest every day, away from our hectic business and three small children. I became accustomed to the easy pace, but it bothered me that I wasn't worth the paycheque I was collecting every Friday, so I decided to earn my keep. I would do the company a special favour. Already having hooked a rug for our wall at home, I knew Mr. 'H' would really appreciate a huge seven foot hanging for his reception area, with the company crest embossed in longer wool and in the company's colours. Darko knew someone who could duplicate their logo onto canvas. The rest was easy.

Mr. 'H' not only loved it, he wanted me to make six more, one for each branch. He actually took it with him to some convention in Calgary. When he returned he had an even better idea.

"Donna, how about if we go into business, approaching big companies, which have famous logos. We can put an ad in the papers advertising for hookers. We could make a fortune. This is a work of art. Companies will jump at it. It'll be a piece of cake." (I got the expression from him.)

"Well, not exactly, you see, I'm just about overwhelmed by all the 'additional sidelines' that I operate. I came here to get some peace and quiet and get away from running numerous businesses, not start another one. Tell you what, Mr. 'H', if I can convince Darko to sell his business, including appliances, vacuums, assorted sundry items, and get a job; then and only then, would I consider this venture — maybe."

It appealed to me because it was all cash-in-advance, not fly now, pay later. Darko's profit was constantly being eaten up through bad debts.

I got to the point, that when a little hair salon wouldn't pay their bill, after dozens of reminders and ten dollars worth of stamps to mail them, I planned to walk into the salon, get my hair done, and when asked to pay, hand an invoice to the proprietor marked PAID IN FULL. He'd be stunned speechless, staring blankly as I walked out with my coiffure.

Going to small claims court was worth more in time and money than these small service calls were worth and I began collecting bad debts in my own way.

Once, Wendy, another really gutsy high school chum, and I, went to a well-known restaurant, right in downtown Toronto, at high noon. We ordered the most expensive and largest meal that we could find on the menu. It was still a little short of what was owing Darko, from two years back, not to mention interest on the money, or overdraft charges which MY bank was charging so I could pay my bills on time. I felt it was the principle of the thing. Can you imagine the commotion when the manager was told we were not going to pay the check and he would have to accept the invoice as payment for our meal? Over fifty patrons watched the fiasco, forks frozen just inches in front of their mouths, trying to hear what was going on. Some came offering to pay if we were short on our check.

"No, he's short, we're full, thanks."

"I'm going to call the police, I'm going to sue you" he yelled, "letting my waitresses and customers know my personal business."

"Better your waitresses find out today that you don't pay up, so they won't be shocked on Friday if they don't get their paycheques." Wendy quipped.

This method of collecting debts started when Darko was once on a ladder, installing a brand new air conditioner, in a butcher's shop. The butcher was already saying it couldn't possibly keep his market cool enough and he felt, labour, time and the unit were only worth $750.00. Darko, having just purchased it for $950.00 (our cost) could take it back to the wholesaler and only lose the 10% restocking penalty and also not have to pay his assistant another $30.00 to help him finish the installation. Known to always stay calm, cool and collected, he started unscrewing and removing the unit. "You no pay, you no get." The butcher, seeing Darko was serious, tried to persuade him to stop dismantling it. Darko ignored him, knowing full well he would never see the $1,100 which the man had agreed to pay, only the day before, especially since he was already making 'half price noises. The butcher called for the 'boys in blue' who then removed Darko from the shop. Since the object was in or on the butcher's premises, only a court order could allow him to remove it.

"Sorry, that's the law."

Darko was furious. "Look, officer, I've been to court once too often, trying to collect from these professional shysters. They order the largest and most expensive units, knowing very well they will never have to pay for it. All they have to do is tell some judge that they aren't satisfied and the judge, come next October or November, will advise me that I can remove my unit. I won't be able to get even three hundred bucks for it by then and they get the use of brand new merchandise, each and every summer. I'm sick of it. They know what they're doing, and they know how to use the law. I either take his $750.00 now or wait six months and end up with a used air conditioner. Either way, since I got out of bed for this turkey this morning, I lose either $980.00 or $230.00. Tomorrow I should stay in bed and not answer the phone, so I don't end up in the poorhouse.

"We sympathize with you sir, but there is nothing we can do. We cannot let you back in there to remove it."

That's when I came up with the idea that if I drove to the butcher's, ordered a side of beef, and had him put it in my trunk; I could refuse to pay and just drive off with it.

"No Ma'am, not really. You cannot use a vehicle to take it from him, without paying. You would have to somehow convince him to deliver the cow to your property, get it inside, then refuse to pay. THAT'S LEGAL. Not exactly kosher, but he would have to sue you to get either the payment or his beef back. You see?"

I did see. Have it delivered. Tell him to send me a bill. Refuse to pay. If he has the nerve to sue me, I'll tell the judge it didn't taste good (actually, that I had made a 'draw' against my husband's account).

As it turned out, that cookie wasn't stupid. Knowing we were going to sue him for the balance anyway, he never paid a red cent. I never got my 'beef' or our money, just a used air conditioner back, seven months later, as predicted. Funny how they never want to return the merchandise immediately, while it's still new. Instead, they wait until their court case, when they inform the judge that they're not satisfied with what they got for 'that much money'.

Collecting was not the only problem or handicap in this business. At 1:00 a.m., taverns would call five companies at the same time. First come, first served. Since customers were dropping two hundred dollars every fifteen minutes on booze, they wouldn't sit without lights longer than absolutely necessary. The other four electricians would then turn around and go back home. More than unscrupulous, but definitely legal.

One night a man drove up to our door and rang the bell at 2:30 a.m. He saw the truck parked in the driveway which advertised 24 hour Emergency Service. "Sorry to bother you folks, would you have one of these fuses by any chance?"

"That'll be seventy-five cents. By the way, since you're here, would you like to buy a washer or dryer?"

We would climb back into bed only to be awakened again at 3:15. "Oh, sorry again folks, hope you weren't asleep yet, it's the wrong amperage. It's really important, we're having a party tomorrow and my wife's got to finish the baking." We stayed up till dawn waiting for him, in case he came back.

Darko had finally had enough of this 'work now, send us a bill' business. I persuaded him to put it up for sale. Armed with his many years of experience of running his own company, the best firms would surely hire him, especially since he was still under forty.

"You'd build up a good pension, seniority and our hospital and medical insurance would be paid. You'd get long weekends, Christmas and Easter off, with pay, EVEN. You won't have to beg people for your hard earned money — they'll be chasing you every Friday with it."

"Sounds good to me. Let's do it. Call an agent to put it up for sale."

You recall how I said our 'Peugot' started a long process of selling cars for a profit. I had met a hair dresser who sold cars on the side like we sold washers. As I was getting my hair treated, he said he had a real bargain parked behind the shop -- "Only $2,200. The blue one. The Pontiac. Go take a look."

TAKE A LOOK? I wasn't ever going to get out from behind the wheel of this car again. It was magnificent, gorgeous; air conditioned, plush interior. The 'WOIKS'! I WANT IT. WHAT A DEAL. I came running back excited.

"Oh ohhh." he notices I'm a little too excited; even for me, about a Pontiac. "I have this feeling, Donna, maybe you found the Cadillac, instead."

"How much?"

"$7,500.00."

"How can you do this to me? I'm in love with the one I was just sitting in. That's the one I'll give you $2,200 for."

"D-A-R-K-O? Can you come over to the salon?", I asked sheepishly, over the phone. "Oh-h-hhh, it's about this great car I just test drove. Do you think the bank would let us have another $5,000 maybe?"

"What's $5,000?" he says "If we're going to go under, then we're going in style."

Now the Caddy, we managed to buy on time — but the gas was pay-as-you-go. I'd had it less than a month when I wanted to give it back.

Looking much younger than a mother of 'three', wise guys at red lights would make comments such as "Daddy loan you the buggy for the night, babes?"

"Don't you know what it takes to go from ten cents to having a Caddy, you turkey?" I'd fume inside.

We did have our fun moments though. On New Year's Eve we had to stop at another emergency service call, on our way to the Big Dance. We drove up in a Caddy. I was in a fur coat, (we figured it was cheaper than pneumonia) my sweetie, the electrician, was in a rented tuxedo. He rang the bell.

"HOW MUCH DO YOU CHARGE?" Her eyes bulged, sorry she'd ever dialed our number.

Mr. 'H' was proud as punch. He had the only secretary with a car bigger than the boss's — until the rust spots appeared. "Donna, a rusty Caddy never impresses anyone."

"Impress?" I was hurt — I don't want to impress. We deserve this car after all the hassle, hard work and lost weekends when we could have been camping instead. We don't want to impress — just enjoy — SOMETHING. Something to make up for our time -- for our efforts.

But hadn't our dreams come true? We had a 'one in a million' marriage. We had 'three in a million' kids. Strangers would come up to me in restaurants, at the courts, in doctor's offices, wherever I took them and comment and congratulate me on my lovely, 'perfectly behaved', little darlings. I was an exceptionally lucky mom. They behaved better than I'd ever dreamed kids could. They were never any trouble.

I had a system. When they did something annoying or that they shouldn't, I would bang something loudly (slipper, roll of paper towels, wooden spoon, anything) that would first get their attention, then proceed even louder to count to three. "ONE! TWO!" They'd freeze, on the spot, like someone turned their switches off, wondering what I might do if they every pushed me to THREE. I didn't know what I'd do either. Thank God I never got past two.

But I MUST be happy??? I had a nice home, a nice, gas-guzzling auto, good jobs -- all of them. Maybe one too many, but we had quality time. Right? Not just quantity. Why was I disappointed in Planet Earth then? Was it because of the crooks who had cheated us since they knew they could get away with it? You mainly needed money in advance if you wanted to sue them. Dozens of other companies, limited companies, were going bankrupt — owing us thousands. We couldn't afford to become limited.

"Daiku, look what came in the mail today. A letter from ABC company's lawyer. He says he's going bankrupt and can't pay the two thousand dollars he owes us. He wasn't limited either. He's in the hospital with a heart condition, the only thing to show after 25 years of hard work. It says he's not skipping the country, as there's no need to. All he's got is a beat up jalopy and an old trailer, with a hole in the roof, which he lives in, poor man."

"Poor man?" He'd really had enough of bad debts.

"Yeah, poor man. I sent him flowers after I read the letter."

"Donna, you're such a sucker for a sob story. Don't tell anyone what you did. They'd laugh you right out of town."

"Hon, if we don't manage to sell this business soon, I'll have a heart condition. Hope somebody out there sends ME flowers — you know?"

"I know. Don't worry, we'll sell it."

I woke the next day with that poor old man in my thoughts. Life's just not fair. It's cold. It's cruel. It's inhumane. Wait a minute — stop that. Self pity's creeping in. Dress the kids -- today's the day Mommy's going to learn how to drive a bike. If you little guys can do 'pop-a-wheelies' down the front steps like that, then surely I could learn to peddle one a few blocks.

The only way I could describe in detail the next eight hours would be to quote from a 'John Gilbert' radio show, where I spent about forty minutes describing in detail, just a few years after the occurrence, what happened that afternoon. They replayed the tape the following weekend and many times after while daily advertising what I would be speaking about. The question and theme for that day's show was; "What would you ask God, if you were to meet Him?" On an impulse, never dreaming I'd get a free line, dialed the radio station's number. "Yes ma'am" said the coordinator "what would you ask Him?"

"Ask Him?" I chuckled, "Oh, I wouldn't ask HIM anything. I don't ever want to meet up with HIM again. Once was enough. I spent a few days in a psychiatric hospital over it. Next time I talk to Him, they'll lock me up for good."

"I had barely, jokingly, finished this amusing statement when I heard John Gilbert's voice, "Yes, go ahead — you're on the air! You say you've M-E-T H-I-M once?"

All of my secretarial training had developed my 'professional voice'. Only over the telephone though. In real life, I want to say so much, so quickly, that they call me "motor mouth". When talking to strangers, in person, I could almost pass out from fright, but telephones were somehow different. My voice was soft, cool, calm, even though I knew thousands were listening to this radio program. I proceeded to relay the most extraordinary and unusual event that I experieneced on that day.

After about thirty days of rain and fog during the entire month of August, it was the first day that had been warm and sunny. A brand new four lane highway had just been built beside the field right next to our house. The road was newly paved, and all the lines were freshly painted, but it was still blocked off to traffic. I climbed on my bike, as I had many times before, and tried to pedal a straight course.

I heard a small voice inside, ever so clearly, say; "Why are you so afraid? You are so full of fear. Don't be afraid — you are in My hands." And with those words, a magnificent presence surrounded me. Actually, it engulfed me. All around me. It was as if I had been swallowed by it. I felt a warm, kind, unbelievable love. It was God. You know when you're in the presence of God. No one has to tell you who it is. He was communicating with me. "Do not fear. Trust Me."

"Trust you? Okay, God, I trust you. If this is You — drive my bike then" and I let go of the handle bars while driving at high speed, directly toward the barricade at the end of the road, my eyes tightly shut. "Let's see what You're going to do." A couple of feet before the barricade, the bike tilted to the left and I landed on the grassy field, still cradling the bike between my legs and still very much aware of this 'power charge' around me. I sat there and just laughed. Could it be? Could this really be happening? It's not going away. Rather, He's not going away.

A very old couple came walking by who had seen me fall and asked if I was all right.

"I'm fine. I just bumped into God. That's all."

I presumed they could see Him too.

I could not VISIBLY see anyone or any being with my eyes and yet I WAS seeing Him. THERE WAS A PRESENCE. My mind's eye saw it. He was enormous — He filled the sky and earth and was definitely there. I climbed back on the bike and rode back and forth on the one mile stretch, questioning what was happening to me. I asked the boys if they could see Him. "God, Mommy? No, I don't see God. Where is He?"

"He's right here. Can't you see Him? Can't you hear Him? He's talking."

"No, mommy."

They thought this was great fun looking for God.

"Well, we are just going to keep biking back and forth till either you do see Him or I don't anymore."

As I rode, I kept looking up at the sun. His brilliance was much greater, stronger. I began to feel the presence of people lining both sides of the road. They were my ancestors. I knew who each one was, even though I had never even heard of some of them. I knew who belonged to which side of the family dating back generations. My grandmother was there too. She was the only one I really did know. I was not seeing shapes but I could feel distinct images. I could have walked up and touched each individual presence. I was too overwhelmed to do anything but keep peddling back and forth between them and whether I rode east or west I was driving toward God. I noticed I felt no sensation. I didn't feel the wind. I couldn't feel the warmth of the sun. I could not tell where my body and limbs ended and where this presence began. We were entwined. I was one with something. It felt like eternity or the infinity of the universe.

Probing my mind and trying to get a grasp on reality or something concrete, the only explanation I could come up with was that sometime during the day I had died. I'd either had a heart attack or died when I fell and I was in purgatory and these relatives, who had been long dead, were going to take me to God. I knew angels were all around. I couldn't feel them or see them but I did have a knowledge that there were many hundreds.

But, if I was in purgatory, why was everything so beautiful, so overwhelmingly lovely and peaceful? I couldn't comprehend the peace. Purgatory was supposed to last for thousands of years — was I going to spend thousands of years pedaling back and forth waiting for God to ACTUALLY appear? What are the kids doing here? Why are they with me if I'm dead? We were obviously in the same state if I could talk to them and they could hear me. THINK. Were we all in a car accident? No, we were on the road riding our bikes. Were we hit by a car? No, all of us couldn't have been hit by one car because we were in different directions all over the road. Surely I would have seen it. Seen something.

As I kept driving I started to feel something leaving and falling off me. As if dirt was dropping off. Sins were falling away. Fears were disappearing. Hate, gossip, as if actual items of clothing, were being shed. I stopped and sat on the grass. This was my judgment. It had to be. Every unkind word I had ever said was being played back to me. Every ugly remark or action was being recalled to my attention and they were melting and fading into oblivion. I sat there wondering if I was supposed to keep peddling.

Something was filling my being as all this garbage was falling away. Love and unexplainable kindness were filling me as burdens and worries and fears were being eliminated, as if forever. The kids joined me on the grass. "When are we going to eat Mom?" I noticed I wasn't hungry. I wasn't thirsty either. Most of all, I didn't even want a cigarette. I felt perfect. This was perfection. Heaven must feel like this. Nothing else could. As we sat there I was being told it was like the Garden of Eden. I felt the presence of wild animals in the shrubs behind me. Lions and giraffes. All tame and at one with the environment.

I sensed that my flesh was going to just tumble off my bones and that my bones would disintegrate into the earth and only my soul or inner being would remain sitting in that spot.

My questions were not being answered but I was accumulating a wealth of knowledge and wisdom. Things I had never even thought about or been interested in, were flooding in my mind, enabling me to understand so much, so quickly. It just poured in. The grass and shrubbery looked greener than I had ever seen it. Colours were unbelievably bright and alive. The clouds and sky were breathtaking. I couldn't still be on earth, even though I could see my house and the familiar neighbourhood. But, I saw evil there. I could feel it. Everything outside this half mile radius wasn't as colourful. It was darker, cooler, dull; didn't have this brilliance. I could tell where paradise ended and the real world began. There were two distinctly different places. I didn't want to go back. I'll just stay here and wait, wait for God or one of His angels to appear.

I hear Him again. "Do you want to go back?"

"No — I don't know. It's evil over there. I want to stay here with You."

At that moment I saw Darko coming through the field waving. HE CAN SEE US! How can he see us? Is he dead too?

"Hi. What are you doing? Am I going to get something to eat?"

I lifted a pebble off the ground. 'Sure, have this." I said handing it to him. "It doesn't matter. We don't need food."

"Let's go get something to eat, I'm starved."

"Darko — can you see Him? Can you hear Him?"

"Who?"

"GOD!"

"Where?"

"Right here."

Puzzled he just stood and stared while Danny and Michael excitedly proceeded to tell him that I had been talking to God all day.

"Can you still see Him, Donna?"

Fear shot through me. If he's here, then we're all dead and he would see Him too. If Darko can't see Him, then I'm still on planet earth, not dead, not in heaven or wherever. What is going on? Is there a choice to be made here? Is that it?

God, don't just take me and the boys. Either take all of us or none of us — PLEASE. If Darko's not coming, let me go back. He couldn't make it without us. Please. Not just us.

I spent twenty minutes explaining how I physically felt nothing. No emotion, just peace. I asked Steve to ride his bike right into me. He smashed hard against my skin.

"Don't do that!" Darko frantically yelled.

"It's okay daddy, she's been letting me do that all day and she says it doesn't hurt."

"Darko, don't you understand? I don't feel that."

I saw a piece of jagged glass on the road and went over and in my bare feet, jumped up and down. Blood was shooting out of my heel. "I can't feel it. I can't feel anything! Please try harder.

Concentrate. Can't you see Him too?" Darko grabbed me by the arm and started to steer me home. I wouldn't give up. He picked me up, threw me over his shoulder, like a caveman, and started to run for home. I struggled to get free. I can't leave here till I find out what's happening. I sensed the evil getting closer as we approached near our yard.

"Let me down. Don't take me back here. Not here!"

He had to put me down inside. He was panting and out of breath. As soon as he relaxed his hold I bolted back out the door and across the field. He chased after me as he screamed over and over: "Someone get an ambulance. Someone get a doctor."

I saw an old white haired lady a couple of hundred feet up the road, walking her collie. I ran over and was petting the dog's head as Darko reached us and in sheer panic pulled my arm away. "Don't do that. He'll bite you!"

The dog growled at him. Now, he knew this was unusual. Dogs would chase me for blocks. I once had to climb on top of a car because a dog was ready to tear me apart. Another time I ran right through the door of a complete stranger's house with a large Great Dane in hot pursuit. They sensed my fear and they would zero in on me from blocks away and then come charging and growling. Any friends we had would have to lock up their dogs when I came over because they acted like they would tear me to shreds, even though they were normally friendly dogs.

He picked me up again, threw me over his shoulders and again started to run for home yelling "Call an ambulance, get some help." The old woman just continued along her way as if there had not been an intrusion.

"Rape! Rape! Help!" I shrieked.

No one paid any attention. Cars passed. Everyone oblivious to the noise and commotion. Darko reached for the phone and again I ran out the door. Back to where I felt safe.

Someone had called the police. The cruiser squealed to a stop. Two officers jumped out and ran toward us, guns drawn.

"NOT ME — HER!" Darko was hysterical.

Since I stood there bruised and bleeding from numerous small cuts, they presumed he was attacking me. Both recognized me from court.

"WHAT'S going on here?"

Darko was completely incoherent, but managed to convince them that I was the one that needed help and not to handcuff him. They looked in my direction puzzled because I looked so calm.

"Is that true Donna? Did you see God? Are you on something?"

"Look guys, you're not going to believe me, so if I'm to go to a hospital I want you to take me to Etobicoke." Then I pointed in the direction of Toronto. "I won't go back that way — ever!" I persisted, pointing in the opposite direction. "I only feel evil over there." They had heard enough.

"Oka-a-ayyy. . . Get in the cruiser, Donna." Then, directing their questions at Darko now, "Is she high on something, or what?"

"Of course not!" Darko exclaimed, now much calmer. "She's never taken drugs."

"I won't get in the car unless you promise to take me that way. pointing to where I felt I'd be safer.

"You know that's not in our jurisdiction. You either get in NOW, or we put you in."

"Okay, okay — don't touch me — I'll get in myself."

During the short ride to the hospital I wondered, what now? Was I insane? Just don't rock any boats — cooperate and wait. Once in Emergency, sitting beside Darko in an adjoining room, I started to shake with cold. That was a good sign. I also ached from the bruises and cuts. Another good sign, I thought. As long as I'm feeling something, I'm back to reality.

Darko said absolutely nothing at all. He just stared in bewilderment until the doctor arrived asking, "What happened?"

Unusual for me, I had nothing to say.

"She didn't want a cigarette. Didn't want to smoke. Insisted she talked to God."

That came out funny. He had brought me to a nut house because I didn't smoke. Was there subtle humour buried somewhere deep inside of Darko? The first time I ever met Darko, I was fifteen, and he offered me a cigarette. He's been trying ever since to get me to quit. I do and he brings me here. No — he was being serious.

"Is she religious?" the doctor continued.

"No she was NEVER religious." came Darko's reply.

My head pivoted in his direction and I belted, "I was always religious!" not understanding why he'd said that. Did he think they would never let me out again if I believed in GOD? Probably.

"Mrs. Martonfi, we can't force you to stay here, but I strongly suggest that you sign yourself in."

"Fine — but I have to be in court next week. You have to let me go to work."

I had to find out what happened. Does this happen to other people? Did I have a nervous breakdown — that lasted only one day?

I was led to a room and given an injection, I didn't wake up for twenty-four hours. I didn't have a phone in my room so I went to the nurses' station, still in my shorts and halter.

"Am I allowed to have a phone here?"

"Yes, if you earn the privilege."

"Could you give me a gown please'?" I asked politely.

"We don't wear gowns — you'll have to send for your own street clothes."

"STREET CLOTHES?"

"I don't have any money or smokes. Am I allowed to smoke?" I'd better be or I'm checking out.
"Absolutely, but not in your room at this time of night."

"If I had some I could sit on the floor in the hall."

I must have sounded either unusually polite or else quite pitiful. She handed me almost a full pack knowing I just got up after a very long sleep and would probably be up for hours.

"Be very quiet — everyone's asleep. You have my permission to go to the lounge and watch TV."

Next morning, I not only had a telephone, I had a pass to leave the psychiatric ward (accompanied) and go to the gift shop. I phoned Darko. His voice bugged me — he sounded pathetic.

"You need money? Your clothes? Make up? Stockings? Curling iron?--- What for?"

If I accumulated enough merit points, they'd let me go to court. Probably in an ambulance, but yes, to court. I explained it was a serious trial and I had no back-up who could go in my place.

"Did you call Mr. 'H'?", I asked, trying to sound reasonable and logical.

"Yes."

Oh I can just imagine what you told him, I thought. You just don't understand. My next call was to Mr. 'H'.

"Donna, you just take all the time you need. Don't hurry back to work. Believe it or not I can manage a while without you." He always sounded like a sweet, understanding, elderly, gentleman, although he was only two years older than me. I wondered where he got his wisdom.

Who should I call next? Friends? No, my friends will understand. I won't have to call them. But wait till the family starts calling — I was now developing some of my own wisdom.

"Nurse, would you have my phone disconnected. I'm going to take advantage of not having to answer dumb questions."

I really like this place. No one knew if you were a patient, doctor or visitor. Everyone in street clothes asking one another, "Are you a visitor?"

"No, I'm a patient, too."

We were all normal. You couldn't tell us apart from the 'outdoor crowd'. Except for the few who were severely depressed, who would stay in their rooms all the time. The 'nervous breakdowns' were in the lounges, freely exchanging stories, laughing or complaining, whichever the case may be. They were concerned for one another. They really felt empathy for one another. They were pleasant. Cracked jokes. I fitted in. I loved it! No wonder my relatives weren't in here. They surely wouldn't let any of them in — this ward is for the normal people to get away from the likes of them. The regular people who weren't vicious, hateful, spiteful — only hurt. Hurt by the morons, the users of society.

Darko appeared, trying to spot me in the large cafeteria we used for recreation between meals.
"Donna, the doors aren't even locked, I just walked in."

I couldn't tell how I was reacting toward him. Everyone here understood my situation — don't you?

"Oh, they only lock the doors late at night to keep you folks out. Never know when someone could walk in and steal our purse or wallet while we're asleep."

His eyes told me this was no time for jokes. He was not amused by any of this.

"I haven't told anyone where you are, just your boss and parents."

Now he was making me angry. "Darko, print it on the front pages of the newspapers. Let the whole world know. I'm not ashamed to be in here. I was like these people, once. Warm, sensitive, I knew how to have a pleasant day. We're all in here only because we're not allowed to be ourselves, let our hair down, spend a day in bed doing nothing when we want to. Always pushed by someone to do or be something we're not. I can relate to these people. I could adopt some and take them home. I've found six aunts, a new mother-in-law and twenty cousins. I wish someone would give me a chance to choose a new family.

"One's had a crippled child, one's husband died of cancer prematurely, another was battered, another's coping with a terminal disease. They're HUMAN. They don't care if my hair is long, green or if I'm bald. Long nails, no nails or each nail painted a different colour. These things don't matter. They're not supposed to matter. Life's too short for that nonsense. I was like that. I used to be ME. Do you understand?"

"I think so, hon. I think so." He left to make arrangements to get my Caddy parked outside. Shortly after I looked up to see Olga, another high school chum approaching from way down the hall. She was carrying one single, long stemmed red rose. My eyes filled with tears. This girl really understood the important things in life. She didn't have to say one word. Bringing me the rose said it all.

I was a little apprehensive about going to translate. I felt a lightheaded weakness, from the medication I guess, that made me feel as if I was in slow motion. Entering the building, I noticed the sergeant of police approaching, directly toward me. I had never actually spoken to him before and wondered if he had anything to do with the case I was there for. He reached for my hand, lifted it and planted a gentle kiss on the top, like in the movies.

"God bless you" he said. Goose bumps appeared as I realized that the news had spread like wildfire and to my astonishment, PEOPLE CARED. They were strangers, yet they cared. The crown attorney, whom I highly respected, stood in front of the witness box as I was being sworn in to 'well and truly translate all such matters...'

"Mrs. Martonfi, has anything happened recently which would interfere with your capability to translate for this court today?" he asked. I looked at him curiously. The warmth of his eyes reinforced my newfound revelation. I was capable. Not of everything, but of many, many things.

"No sir, nothing's happened, I'm capable." I replied in a tone that said, "Thank you."

I readmitted myself well before 5:00 p.m. I didn't want to break any rules or lose privileges. I took a short nap before supper. Knowing many 'night hawks', such as myself, who enjoyed company into the wee hours, I suggested we order a pizza around midnight. Everyone instantly got excited. We checked with the nurses' station. "Sure, if you're hungry — it's fine with us.

Three or four people ran around collecting 75 cents from each person. Putting on my 'professional voice', I phoned the winning pizza place. "I'd like to order seven large pizzas. Two with everything on it, hold the anchovies on four and one just basic. Thank you."

"Where would you like them delivered, Ma'am?"

"Local Hospital, Psychiatric Ward" — and then, realizing he was about to hang up the receiver — "NO, no, this is not a crank call. Call the number, ask for the nursing station, they'll confirm our order. Please. We're hungry."

The first pizza party went better than expected. In the week that followed, that little pizza place doubled its business. The hospital staff, realizing the positive influence, joined in our Midnight Madness. We rechristened the hospital the 'Hilton'.

I grew daily. Parents weren't around to inquire why we were hungry — Hadn't I cooked enough supper for Darko and myself — I should cook more and not live on this garbage. Look at me, anyone could see I'd wasted away since I'd taken up my own kitchen... "Haven't you noticed, I'm ten pounds heavier and Darko's forty-five pounds heavier since we set up shop?"

Our motto: Do your own thing. If someone doesn't like it, they know what they can do. I WAS CERTIFIED SANE. Un-admitted. STRONGER and even more DETERMINED to block out people and parts of the world which didn't quite agree.

Anna came for a visit my first week home. "Donna, what are you doing, spring cleaning?" she laughed seeing the mess.

"I'm cleaning up my house, Anna. I'm cleaning up my life." Those were words she remembered for years and years. Anna brought up this statement as I was reading her the rough draft of this book.

"Donna, you have to put that in. I remember so vividly. I can hear you saying it. Many times I've thought over the years, YES — YOU DID... you certainly did."

To make the day even more memorable still, I had run out of sugar. We ended up putting strawberry jam in our coffee. It tasted not too bad. You wouldn't have caught me doing anything this abnormal had I not spent two weeks at the Hilton. I could tell Anna was impressed. I had remembered how to have fun, just like we did in high school; no reservations. Even if it's different -- it's OK -- go for it -— do it!

Verna, a very charming, classy lady, who lived not many doors away, stopped in to see if she could do anything. I'd only met her once before, when she was canvassing for the Cancer Society, but I had noticed her and her husband, many times, when they drove past my house, as I watched through the kitchen window, while doing dishes.

"Why don't you come to church with me on Sunday, Donna?"

"C-H-U-R-C-H? Sunday's the only day I have to sleep in and then do the weekly cleaning. I couldn't, ever. What for?"

"Things are happening over there, you wouldn't believe it, Donna. Why don't you come for Bible study on Tuesday night?" she gently persisted.

B-I-B-L-E S-T-U-D-Y? Is she kidding? If it's got to do with the Bible, it's got to be corny. This gal's square, I thought — yet, I still really liked her. Can't believe anyone with this much class goes to Bible study.

"Thanks, but — no thanks."

"Well, I think I'll be going, if you'd like to take a swim, you and the boys; just come on over."

"Now, on that, I will take you up. I can't swim but they've taken lessons; swim like two little fish. Thank you."

Baka Sisa was now convinced I was totally insane. "I don't want the boys calling me Baka Sisa. I want you all to call me Baka, only. Sisa is Maria's name, not mine."

Too bad, you're stuck with it now. You're lucky that's all we call you. When you call me by my correct name, either one, and can spell the names of your grandchildren properly, we'll discuss it again.

She had built up a new-found authoritarian attitude.

Danny and Michael's school had a class for specifically handicapped children. At recess, they would play with and protect a particular little boy, also named Michael. The teachers noticed the improvement in Michael 'C' immediately, his response to being with 'Nanny' and 'Ickle', as he called them. They asked if I would give permission for the three boys to be photographed playing together. The society for the mentally retarded wanted to make a poster entitled "FRIENDSHIP IS" and circulate it among libraries and schools coast to coast. I was honored. To think my boys actually did relate to the quality of life that I tried to instill in them. I couldn't wait to see the poster. Darko felt the same -- a proud POPPA.

Baka Sisa was another story. "Darko, you can't let her continue with this. People will think your children are retarded too. It'll haunt them later in life, when they go to university. They won't be able to prove they're not crazy." I have chosen to clean up her actual statements. Darko ignored her.

"Donna, why does she bother you so much? Ignore her. She's primitive beyond words. We do what we want to whether she likes it or not. We can't change her."

The same weekend she took the kids to Niagara Falls. Darko and I would meet them there on Sunday and drive back together. Dan and Mike ran up to me as soon as they spotted me.

"Mommy, you know what she said about you? She said you were crazy, that we should never listen to you. That you were nuts. Daddy was okay until he met you and now he's crazy too -- like you. Tell him Mom, tell him what she said."

I saved it. Saved it for 95 miles. I could choose my words carefully while driving home and then drop the bomb. She chattered busily about how much she'd spent on them, all the things she'd done for them, all the way back not knowing I was aware of her purpose for this excursion. Darko was aware. Upon entering, he asked his father if he would sit down, not interfere and listen to what I had to say, then, he could throw us out.

I calmly and sternly started my thirty minute lecture, with everyone present.

"These children love me and their father. They are not forced to love or respect us. It comes naturally. This is the result of my system of upbringing. They are not to be told not to trust us. They are not to be told we are crazy or wish them harm. They are not to be told to keep things from us, such as you have asked them to do about this little episode. They are at an impressionable age, so therefore, unless you encourage your grandchildren to love, honour and obey us, you will not set eyes on them again; till they are at least eighteen. They have been taught they can freely come to us and trust us, with any problems or difficulties which arise and they will not be punished, but rather encouraged. If you persist in interfering with my methods or tactics, you will be forbidden to see them, unchaperoned. As for my sanity, I have five times the I.Q. of anyone you surround yourself with and have therefore been let loose, back into society. I do not ask that you agree with me or that you believe me, but I do insist that you be at least cordial and conduct yourself civilly in my presence or the children's. Any thoughts that you have about my sanity or your son's, or the way I choose to bring up my children, or any opinions you have as to the rearing of these children, you will keep to yourself when in our company. You will never dispute anything I say when in their presence. I refuse to further discuss this matter and intend to never have to ever again. Is that clear?"

My father-in-law looked impressed. Baka Sisa, dazed. I doubted whether any of this had really registered, but I could tell she knew I meant business. She knew she had ruffled nature's 'protective motherly instinct' and that I could kill if there was any question of our boy's balance being upset.

Chapter Six

A VERY LONG HORROR STORY

Matters were now in pretty good shape. We had sold the business and half the money went to pay the $15,000 demand loan at the bank. The additional $15,000 we owed was a chattel mortgage, payable in five years. Darko applied and was accepted as an electrician at a major automotive company. Paycheques were much higher than we were accustomed to. Also, the road in front of our home was being widened to a four lane highway with two ,additional turning lanes directly in front of our driveway. The community was fighting the expropriation but everyone knew, you can't stop city hall. We then fought for more money, because the sum they offered did not compensate for the depreciation of our homes.

One morning I woke to a noise which quickly sent me running to the front door. A city worker was cutting down our 35 foot blue spruce. I ran out and unplugged his buzz saw. "What are you doing?"

"It's okay, city fix — city pay." He tried reasoning in broken English.

"City fix nothing — city pay nothing —get off my property." I demanded. Had the city paid me anything I would be able to move the spruce and maple trees. Trees were worth more than silver and gold to me. He immediately left. I assessed the damage. I had stopped him just in time.

The same evening I was served with a 'Restraining Order' which stated that if I interfered with the work crew again, I would be arrested and taken to jail. JAIL? Because I wanted to save two trees and have them relocated? Along with the notice was a cheque for $7,000.00.

I had the cash now but I didn't have a property to move the trees to and so I watched sadly from the window as my trees came down. The construction in front of our home was soon in full swing, going strong. There was a mountain of dirt as high as our roof and we had to park three blocks away to carry our groceries home.

"Let's sell the house Donna, and move to the country. Let's really start enjoying a home, enjoying our life."

"Sounds good to me — it's about time we have some peace and quiet." My heart was overjoyed at the prospect of moving to the country. "It'll be like going home to a cottage every night. We're going to make this dream come true yet."

Ben was the real estate agent of all agents. He must have covered half of southern Ontario with me.

I wanted a lot for a very little. One day he drove up excited beyond words. "I've found it! This is the one," he sputtered, jumping around. Taking one look at the picture, I knew instantly; "I can't afford that, Ben."

It included over an acre of land, just outside of Milton, 3,300 square feet, five bedrooms, family room with fireplace, a twenty-seven foot kitchen, drop ceiling lighting, central air and central vacuum. It was vacant. I noticed the price was blotted out.

"You can, you can, let's go quick, get the kids in the car, you're buying this house today."

Well I didn't realize how big 3,300 square feet was until I stood in front of this mansion. "In a million years I couldn't afford this, Ben."

"Just go inside — take a look."

What a shock — it was in shambles. The main construction was ideal, but what a mess. "The house has been rented for ten years, off and on. The last family ruined it so badly the owner's willing to let it go cheap." I was overwhelmed. I could afford it. If I knocked off an additional $20,000, it would be within our reach. We'd fix it up, over time.

Each time he opened one of the bedrooms upstairs, I thought I was seeing the master bedroom, they got larger and larger. When he did open the master, I walked onto a football field. The change room was the size of the boys' present bedroom and led to an ensuite bathroom. "Hurry!" I began getting excited; he was already doing a jig.

"Let's go get Darko, but Ben, you have to promise me you'll calm down, not say one word. Let me talk to Darko. You don't know him well. He has to think this house is HIS idea."

"As long as you put in an offer, you won't know I'm in the same room or that I'm in sales."

"Darko, Ben's here for coffee. We just looked at this big barn of a house, on an acre of land, about thirty minutes from here."

His ears perked up, "Big barn?" (We had sold the business, but we hadn't sold the appliances, vacuums, motors, tools, junk, etc.)

"Darko, it's a mess inside. Broken windows. Hole in the kitchen floor. Kitchen cupboards just dangling from hinges."

Now he's in the car. Ben's shooting me terrified looks through the rear view mirror. Don't worry Ben, I know this guy. He wouldn't be in the car if he thought it was 'my kind of house'. He was afraid he'd have a sunken tub, sunken living room, finished rec room and NO BARN. He needs room for his junk.

"Donna, this can all be repaired. We'll buy new bathroom fixtures and cover the kitchen and halls with ceramics. You'll see — I'll make it beautiful. We'll be able to get twice the money when I'm finished with it."

By this time I was surprised Ben wasn't laying on the floor playing dead. He had a lot to learn about sales pitches.

"Donna, you've just got to get into real estate. I've never seen anyone operate like that."

"I just know my buyer, Ben, that's all. I know what does and doesn't appeal to Darko. He wouldn't have got in the car if he saw I was nuts about it — that would surely mean it wasn't his style."

I hadn't even noticed we didn't have one mature tree on the entire acre. Darko promised we'd plant a living fence of cedars all around the property.

A stipulation of the offer was that we would have the keys two weeks in advance and have access to renovate.

"It's not a wise move, Donna, never recommended. Money hasn't changed hands; not a good idea." He gave up, seeing I was a 'do it yesterday, not tomorrow' type. The Credit Union was giving us a mortgage large enough to handle the additional expense of improvements.

We did a super job. Very professional.

Two days before closing, I was asked, through my lawyer, by the owner, to return the keys. That's strange. Why return them just to have them handed back the next day? My criminal mind, through hearing so many court cases, decided I should make an extra set, just in case something went wrong. Fortunately my female intuition paid off. We were sitting in the lawyer's office, accompanied by both agents, and the owner. He discovered he had undersold. He wanted an additional $40,000.

"No way!" Darko and I blurted out. We had just spent close to $25,000 on improvements. That's why it looks so great. Our own money was spent to improve the property.

It didn't matter, he decided not to sell.

"He can't do that, he signed our offer." we protested.

"Well, yes, legally we could sue him to get the costs back, but no one could force him to sell if he didn't want to."

"But I want that house. I don't want to spend years in court getting our money back."

The entourage left. "Ben, step outside. I don't want you to hear what I'm planning." I then continued. "Isn't possession 9/10 of the law?"

"You can't break-in Donna, you'll be arrested." my lawyer cautioned.

"Who said anything about breaking in? I'll keep in touch."

One hour later I phoned my lawyer back; "Don, you may inform the other lawyer we have possession. Tell them to sue US if they want US out. I had duplicate keys cut."

I don't think Don realized he had a client that would set precedents. There's always a way to beat the system. I was learning fast.

"She can't do this. There's got to be a law! Get a sheriff to evict her!" yelled the owner.

"I'm sorry, but you'll just have to sue her, which might take years and you'll lose anyway because we have a signed offer stating she can purchase the premises for the stipulated price. So-o-o sorry."
For three and a half months that man tried to get us evicted.
"But she hasn't even paid a cent. How can she have possession and live for free?"

"Anytime you want payment, the mortgage cheque is ready to be picked up. Oh yes, one more thing, you've made her so angry and she's suffered so much mental anguish and additional legal expense, she's now offering to pay YOU $40,000 less. A frozen mortgage, you understand, payable in twenty years, without interest accumulating. A token of your good faith. Found the premises in worse shape than they had first appeared to the naked eye. Take it or leave it. The option is yours."

The frozen token of faith money allowed us to carry the payments of the other property, without having to sell it before the road was completed; leaving it as a future investment while rented out. This allowed us to trade our gas guzzling Caddy for a small brand new sports car.

At this point, I should explain how I ended up with two automobiles . . . At the dealer, sometime in October or November, Darko and I had ordered a white and maroon Omni Hatch back with a sun roof; a four on the floor beauty. When we went to take delivery just before Christmas, there was a bright yellow and black sports coupe with large black letters, 024, written all over it and it had plaid seats. All I need was a racing helmet to top it off. It was cute, but certainly not a very feminine looking car for my new profession.

I was going into real estate. KNEW ALL ABOUT IT, just from the experience of my last purchase. I quit my job and enrolled in real estate school. Remember the gal who got me into translating? I replaced myself with Jan, as I knew she'd get along great with Mr. 'H' and the new Vice President.

I joined Ben at the company he worked for, eager and ready to give it my all.

I laughed when I saw my 024. "This car clashes with my personality."

"Sorry Ma'am, you have to take either this one or wait till the New Year for your order. There's a backlog for Omnis."

WAIT? I never did know what that word meant. "I'll take it. I've driven stranger things. It kind of grows on you. At least it's brand new,so there won't be any mechanical problems for at least a couple of years."

As fate would have it, the first time I came in for service, my original order was there, with my name on the order slip.

"Why can't I just switch them? This one's beautiful. A lady's car. I feel like a 'hood' driving the other."

"We can't do that, but why not give 024 to your hubby and buy this one also?"

"Darko, why not? It's Valentine's Day. What a gift! It even looks like a valentine." I have a way of backing him into a corner when it comes to cars, but he really liked the idea of two identical ones (although as different as night and day) and was already aware of the gas saving. So-o-o we traded in the truck and I drove off in my four wheel valentine.

The Horrors Start

By this point we had two mortgages on the old house, two (one frozen) on the new, and payments on two brand new cars. We wouldn't be too bad off if we could just rent the property and at least cover one of the mortgages. The other three only amounted to $30,000, with no payments needing to be made on the $40,000 token. It would have been easy if the construction had ceased. Not too many people are willing to live on a main highway behind a mountain of dirt. Just as luck would have it, Darko was laid off, indefinitely. Now what? No pay cheques for either of us. we had: four mortgages, two car payments, and three kids.

Shortly after Darko was laid off, he woke in the middle of the night screaming with pain. I rushed him to the hospital where he was given a shot of cortisone and sent home. For five weeks he crawled around the house on his hands and knees, unable to stand on his feet from the pain in his ankles. He had gout, a form of arthritis which affects the joints.

I worked harder and sold ten homes in my first six months. I just had to wait for the deals to close before I got some nice, fat pay cheques. I mean — I put in the time, the gas, drew up offers, presented them and negotiated sales. I should get paid, right?

First deal: I didn't get paid. Being too naive, the Mickey Mouse company said, "Prove you rented the home, we'll send you your cheque." (The agent had done me a favour and typed the offer himself seeing how I was new in the business and neglected to put my name and my company's name as the co-agents on the offer.)

Second deal: I didn't get paid. Another very crooked, Mickey Mouse company, brought my vendor an offer which they back-dated three weeks. Since he desperately needed the sale, and since he was only looking out for himself, I was totally cut out of this illegal document and the sale appeared as if it was finalized three days before my listing became effective.

Third deal: I didn't get paid. The buyers didn't qualify for the mortgage because they had gone into their own business and couldn't prove their income.

In the end, I only got paid for four deals out of ten. Not to fret! I was paying my dues — learning my lessons — all this was going to make me a better agent in the end.

"Donna, you're jinxed. I've been in real estate twenty years and didn't lose six deals. Everything happens to you. Can't understand how you can still walk around with a smile on your face." Those were just some of the comments at the office from the other agents.

"I'm hoping if I ignore it, it'll all go away." I'd reply.

But it wasn't going away. It got worse. I came home one day to a 'demand notice' from the Internal Revenue. They were demanding twelve thousand dollars in back taxes, owing for 1977.

"But sir, we won't get payment for the sale of our business until 1982."

"Sorry Ma'am," (I was haunted by this phrase everywhere I went, nothing good ever followed 'sorry ma'am') "the documents were signed in '77. There's nothing we can do. The twelve thousand is due and payable immediately. Take out a bank loan."

"No bank in the world would give me another red cent. We're mortgaged to the hilt."

"Then I'm afraid we'll have to garnishee your husband's wages."

"Wages? What wages? When he was working seven days a week, twelve hours a day, you deducted $500 a week in taxes. Now he receives less than $200 from pogie. Just send back what he's put in." I was close to hysteria.

What next? I couldn't take another incident.

"I'm afraid it just doesn't work that way. You'll receive a refund next April for the weekly overpayment. It'll average out."

"What do I do till April? I have to eat. I can't just sit and wait for the money!"

"I'm sorry, we'll only give you an additional thirty days."

He didn't sound concerned at all. What was thirty days? Who could produce twelve thousand dollars in thirty days? If he had given me a year, it wouldn't be enough to come up with that kind of money.

Relating my newest problems at the office the next day, I was invited to go to a really good fortune teller. It was the 'in' thing. Everyone was going. Why not, I thought? I had to find out when all of this was going to stop.

That incident began the first of regular weekly visits. The more accurate the tellers were, the more people came along, the more psychics they recommended, and so on.

I was really feeling jinxed. Just everything was going wrong. One Friday, the thirteenth, I wondered if I should even get out of bed. On the way to meet Darko for a coffee date close to the office, a truck directly in front of me rolled over on its side, for absolutely no reason. Driving at eighty km/h, I narrowly escaped a pile up. Fortunately, I never follow too closely. I stopped my car and assisted the driver to his feet, wondering if I should proceed any further.

Don't be silly. This was a nasty coincidence. Darko would be waiting. I walked into the restaurant, seated myself, and proceeded to tell Darko the story of my close call. A waitress, who was familiar with my habit of pouring water in my coffee to cool it off, approached with a glass. When she placed it on the table, it tilted and soaked my skirt.

"Don't worry, it's only water, it'll dry." I insisted.

She brought another glass and the same thing happened again. Now I was saturated AND worried. She was an older lady, too old for pranks and too good a waitress. "Never mind the water, just bring the coffee, I'll drink it hot."

The customers were really chuckling, especially since it was Friday the thirteenth. As she brought the coffee, apologizing profoundly, I saw the cup slipping off the saucer and moved like a bolt of lightning out of my seat. The other patrons were rolling on the floor laughing, choking on their food. They must have thought this was a comedy routine. Coffee was all over the table. I was not laughing.

Is there such a thing as bad luck? Curses? "Lady, go home. Don't get out of bed till tomorrow." they ribbed me. "This is definitely not going to be one of your days."

"I have to go see a good psychic, one that knows about bad luck," I exclaimed, chills running through me.

"Donna, these are not normal occurrences you're constantly experiencing. Go to someone good", was the general opinion at the office. Except for Joe; he was the exception. He took me aside and said, "Donna, pray. Pray like you've never prayed."

"I do, Joe. I do. It doesn't help."

"Then go to church." he advised. I was stunned. I imagined Joe disco dancing, partying, doing anything but going to church.

"Are you serious? I can't picture you going to church."

"A good Italian boy like me? Of course I go to church. My wife goes with the kids, every Sunday. Try it. It can't hurt."

Can't help either, I thought, but the fact that he would talk to me like that really moved me. I saw him in a different light. I had always respected and admired Joe and the type of agent he was, but I realized now that he had some hidden quality. That's what I'd senced all along.

Sure enough, that day I was also directed to a particular psychic who was recommended as being one of the best. He was mucho expensive too! Only a few friends came along.

"Yes, you definitely have a curse on you. I can see it surrounding your home and family. No problem, here's what to do. You have to collect holy water from three Catholic churches. They have to be named after male saints. When you mix all the water together, you have to sprinkle each and every corner of your house while you say the Apostle's Creed. You must do this right at midnight every night for twelve nights."

I was a rational, mature grown up. Was I going to fall for this rubbish? The girls with me were told some pretty amazing facts about their past. This guy had even been on TV. Police used him as a last resort to solve a missing child caper. Of course I was going to fall for it — everyone else did; besides, he was Catholic — it had to be okay.

I don't know if you're familiar with the Apostle's Creed, but it just has to be one of the longest prayers out there. A 3,300 square foot home has quite a few corners, too. This was not going to be an easy fete.

I have neglected also to mention up to this point, that we had a Doberman living in our garage. I thought I could get over my fear of dogs. If I could get used to him, I wouldn't be afraid of anything, ever again. I was fine when my kids were around, but no way was I going to stand beside him, in the garage, at midnight, doing 'hocus-pocus'; not in a million years!

Darko by then had been hired temporarily by another company — STEADY MIDNIGHTS! So, that complicated matters. This 'midnight prayer vigil' was not going to work out. I was scared out of my mind. I was literally frightened of my own shadow. Jumpy. Nervous. I thought my heart was going to leap out of my chest by the time I finished 'blessing' the corners of the basement each night. I thought I could feel evil. I always felt an eerie presence. To make matters worse, when I told the psychic I wasn't doing the garage, he insisted that each square inch had to be exorcised if it was going to work.

A few days later Darko came home, still a little shaky from his experience. Both my tires blew out, simultaneously. I barely managed to get the car under control without killing myself."

We were now without a set of wheels, while we waited for the radials. Not three days after we had the 024 back, new tires and all, Darko bolted through the front door, really upset this time.

"You're not going to believe what happened today. Joe and I were driving along when an explosion, like a sonic boom, stopped me in my tracks. It was in the car. We got out and then saw the glass of the hatch back had shattered into a million pieces. Donna, it looked like a mosaic."

"Oh Darko, I'm getting scared. Something out there is after us.

"I know, I know. The dealer said it has never happened in the history of Omnis. He thought I hit it with a hammer. Fortunately there wasn't a hole anywhere. Not from a stone or anything. Right after he looked at it, it just went THUMP and all those pieces of glass caved into the back. You should have heard the initial bang. I actually looked for a bullet hole."

I showed up at the office, smiling as usual. "Donna, a new year's coming. Things'll change for you. You'll see." Everyone was really concerned. We had become walking catastrophes.

Coming home one evening, upon entering the kitchen, we were horrified to find our whole ensuite shower on top of the kitchen stove. There was a hole in the ceiling that a large person could climb through. It just caved through. I didn't even clean up the mess. I just went upstairs and waited for midnight. No use worrying, we can't afford to get it fixed. Ignore the hole and use the main bathroom. The very next morning, I was standing in the shower, and I froze motionless. "D-D-D-a-a-r-r-k-k-o! L-o-o-k! Come quick!" The tiles above the tub in which I was standing were popping (not falling off as if they were rotten, but actually plinging) off the wall, hitting the shower curtain on the opposite side.

"GET OUT OF THERE, QUICK!" he yelled.

"Darko - they're not rotten. The house is only eleven years old and they were actually popping off."

"I saw," he said, worry written all over his face.

"How am I going to wash so I can go to work?"

"Wash in the kitchen sink, like you did the kids when they were little."

Can you imagine standing in a kitchen sink, trying to wash your feet in ice cold water, so you can go to work?

"Darko, there's no hot water." Of course there wasn't, the bottom had fallen out of our hot water tank.

Was I getting scared? You bet your boots I was. Especially while driving home a few nights later. The streets were a sheet of black ice. I was cautiously coming over the top of a hill, only a few miles from my house, ignoring the parade of cars impatiently piling behind me, oblivious to the hazardous ice under their wheels. As I topped the slope I panicked when I saw about five people, on their hands and knees, all over the pavement. I rode the clutch and turned the wheel to the left, mounted a snowbank and came to a stop behind a tree on the farmer's field. I put on my hazard lights to warn the oncoming traffic. All sixteen cars piled up in a colossal accident, with telephone poles and hydro poles coming down, making the road completely impassible. Mine was the only car not damaged.

By now I was convinced something was after me, but I couldn't understand how I managed to avoid being injured in all these calamities.

I went back to the psychic. "Things are worse," I cried.

"You have to bless your garage. You must. You'll only be frightened for another three nights and then you'll never be frightened of anything again."

I held onto this promise. Darko had the weekend off, and on the third night he had to go back to work. By the time I'd zoomed through the basement, first floor, garage and second floor, I was breathless. Never be afraid of anything after tonight. That's a relief!

Sitting there on my bed, watching TV, I heard the most eerie noise coming down the hall. I froze. Chills engulfed me. It was coming from Dan's room. Sort of a groaning, moaning, talking. He must be talking in his sleep. BUT THIS DIDN'T SOUND like garbled talk. Sounded spooky, like in horror movies. Across the hall, from Mike's room, came the reply, in the same horrendous eerie tone. They were communicating back and forth, in turn. I must stress that they were by no means awake or pulling pranks. I did not move a muscle or even blink. I was frozen with fear, waiting for the floor to open up and hell itself to swallow me alive.

"God help me! HELP ME!" I was still sitting shaking in the morning, with my nails pressed so hard into the palms of my hands they were bleeding.

Oh, he was right. After last night, NOTHING was going to scare me like that again, not like THAT!

During the following week, I sensed a premonition that I needed a black suit for someone's funeral. The feeling was so strong that I went out and bought one. When we found the Doberman dead in our garage, I not only cried uncontrollably, but also felt foolish that this was why I needed the suit. The very next day my mother notified me Zandar had died.

Now I really believed in premonitions. "We'll all go to the funeral in one car and then spend the night in a hotel."

Standing in front of the open casket, tears streaming down my face, I prayed for her soul. For the first time in my life, she didn't frighten me. She looked peaceful, not mean. Amazingly, the people that knew her closely respected her. I thought, "Had you lived with her twenty-five years ago, you wouldn't even be here". Everyone worried how my uncle was going to manage without her. Rest in peace, Zandar.

It was the New Year. I was back at the psychic. What next? "You will be changing companies. I see the letter 'J'."

Yes, I had been approached by a small broker to become an associate. The letter even fit. What does the name 'Mile' mean to you?"

"Oh, that must be Millie. She's an agent at my office. We've known each other since high school."

"Very prominent. Also, by the time you are thirty-six, you will be living in Pasadena, with a man named John. He'll be involved with horses; either racing or training them."

It can't be. The other fortune teller had told me those same three facts. The one that communicated with a Chinese ghost. She was Chris's mother's friend for years and was very rarely wrong.

"But my husband and I are inseparable. Everyone calls us 'the clones'. We'd never split up."

"I'm not talking about splitting up. By the time you're thirty-six, you'll be a widow and already remarried."

I came back to the office and told Millie and Joe what this guy had said. I'm to quit here and take the position with 'J'. Things just have to get better and I'm not even going to think about being a widow. I won't hear of it!

"Do you think it's a wise move, Joe? I just have to make some real money. The Income Tax people have given me two extensions already and they're really pushing. Could changing companies hurt?"

"You won't know unless you try Donna. I wish you the best. Good luck." he replied.

When I phoned Chris to tell her that her mother's friend, Samara, and both of my other psychics, had said the same thing, she offered to help. Since the Internal Revenue was still on my back, she and Hank had agreed to lend us $7,000. What a pet! No one in my life had ever offered help before.

"Thanks Chris, but I can't take your money. Besides, $7,000 is just a drop in the bucket. I'm behind on all my payments and that's only half of what I owe the IRS anyway."

"If you send them something at least, maybe they'll stop harassing you for another six months. Take it, please. Not only that, but Hank and I have decided to buy a house, so if you sell our condo and we buy a home, that'll be so much more towards your debt."

I was really touched. Things were looking better. A new, hopefully better, real estate office, $7,000, plus two potential deals. When I offered the revenue department only half of the money and cried all over the man's desk, relating my sob story, he agreed to give me more time for the rest.

Were things getting better? No, not at all.

Chris called in the middle of one night. "We'd like our money back as soon as possible, Donna."

"What? Why? I don't have it."

"I spoke to Samara, and she said you're never going to pay us the money back and things are going to get worse for you. She said we've kissed our money goodbye. Hank is worried sick. It's taken us seven years to save it up. I'm just sick over this."

"Don't worry Chris. If I do anything, I'll get your money back to you. I promise. What else did she say?"

"I really don't want to tell you, Donna. None of it was good."

I woke Darko up and filled him in.

"We'll have to get a loan somewhere; from somebody. They're going to lose sleep over this, till they see that cheque. Then we'll have to let go and give up."

"Let go?"

"Yes. Of everything. I'm frightened for the lives of the kids. This has to stop. We have to let go of the house, the cars, the fridge, the stove, everything. As long as we have the kids and each other, they can have the rest. Nothing else matters but US. We can start over. It'll be easier than trying to pay off $206,000. We might not work as hard the second time around, but it's not important any more, you know?"

"I know, darling, I know. There's nothing more we can do. The harder I work, the further in the hole we get. We're throwing $100,000 in equity out the window. That's a lifetime."

"I'm convinced the devil himself is out to get us Darko."

As I said that, my kitchen cupboard flew open and we turned in time to see the ceramic cooking pot, which was at the bottom of a pile of plastic bowls, fly out to the middle of the kitchen, right above our heads, not disturbing the bowls that were piled on top of it, and shatter in a million, trillion, pieces, with a loud BANG.

All that remained was a powdery residue. No pieces or chunks, just powder.

We ignored it. We continued talking, emotionless, as if nothing had happened. I didn't even stop to clean up the mess before we went upstairs to bed. It was all too much.

I felt I had a high mountain in front of me. I had tried to climb over it, crawl under it, go around and through it. I had never passively stood still. Finally, I'd come to an impasse -- a dead stop. It was just too insurmountable.

"I GIVE UP!!!"

Chapter Seven

CLOSE ENCOUNTERS WITH THE LIVING GOD

It was a pleasant February, without any blizzards. I had received an offer on an out-of-town property that I had recently listed. It was from Sue, an agent from my previous office, one of the 'psychic jet set'. She had left just shortly after I did.

"Since it's so far away, why don't we drive out together in one car?"

I'm not trying to say the nicest things about all my friends, but they are all gorgeous, especially this one. Her face was a work of art. She was tall, slender, with each hair in place and her make-up was superb. She looked better than any fashion model I had ever seen. I couldn't figure out why she wasn't modeling.

"How have you been, Sue? I've heard things aren't going very well, that you've been unhappy."

"Not going well? Unhappy? Are you kidding? I've never been happier in my entire life!" She proceeded to tell me about becoming 'Born Again' and having a personal relationship with Jesus Christ. I couldn't believe my ears. Here was someone who went to a church where they all believed they walked and talked with God Almighty; just as I had, that day on the road.

"Everyone at your church believes this?"

"Yes. He's REAL. He rose from the dead. Where do you think He went?"

"Well, I don't know. I've never thought about it. I've never considered Jesus as risen and alive. I've only thought of Him as either hanging on a cross, or else as a small baby, in His mother's arms, on Christmas Day.

"As soon as we're finished here, we're going to drive to a bookstore and buy you a Bible."

"BIBLE?" That word bothered me. Fairytales. Jonah swallowed by a whale or something. But, I was becoming curious. I had never read one or owned one. "Okay," I agreed.

She continued, "Donna, oh if you could only come to see me be baptized. Nobody else I know will be there. Please."

"Baptized?" I laughed, "At your age?"

"You have to be immersed in water like Jesus was, not just have it sprinkled on you, and it has to be a decision that you yourself make, not your parents. That doesn't count."

I didn't know why, but I wasn't considering her a 'Jesus Freak' or a 'Bible Thumper'. She was one of the most 'with it', up to date people around. What she was saying made sense. A lot of sense. I was taught that Christ rose from the dead, but not that He was actually alive. Could He talk? Why not? The majority of people I knew partially believed in God. If He WAS there, and did create all this, why not talk to His creation? He did once, to me.

"I'll have to check with a priest, Sue. I don't think Catholics are allowed to go into other churches."

We finished the business end of our trip and proceeded to find a Bible. She carried hers in her purse. No, still a bit too corny, a big one will do.

I was surprised to find it only cost about nine dollars. Don't know why I'd imagined all Bibles had to cost seventy-five dollars or more.

"Are you certain this is the same Bible that Catholics read?" I asked the cashier.

"Yes of course, Miss. It's a Christian Bible."

I rushed home and phoned a priest. "Could I go and see a friend baptized in a nondenominational church?"
"Yes, of course you may," came the reply. I was actually surprised.

Sunday night arrived. The church was packed. I seated myself near the back with Dan and Stevie. I was amazed by the simplicity of it. I looked up to see a water tank above the altar; waiting for full grown adults to be immersed.

The service started. . . nothing unusual. I presumed the man speaking, wearing the three piece suit, was the priest. It was very, very informal, not pompous at all. Another man dressed in a black gown appeared in the water tank and about a dozen people entered the tank, one by one, as the minister baptized them in the name of the Father, the Son and the Holy Ghost. Each told a short account of running into the Living God and what it had done for their lives.

The organ was playing magnificently soothing music, not Gospel Hymns, which always did bug me, but a mellow, ballad type rhythm. One song was:

'Holy Spirit, Thou are welcome in this place,
Omnipotent Father of mercy and grace,
Thou are welcome in this place.'

Everyone in the congregation was singing thunderously.

That's when it happened. My hair, almost down to my waist, shot straight out of my head. Startled, I reached up. It wasn't sticking out. But I could feel it standing straight out of my head and I felt each strand as if I'd stuck my finger in a light socket and I knew exactly how many I had. A saying I half remembered whisper through my head, something about God knowing every hair of your head. Well I knew too at that moment. No one noticed my dilemma. Their arms were raised, their eyes closed, singing, "Sweet Holy Spirit, Sweet Heavenly Dove, Stay Right Here With Us, Filling Us With Your Love".

My mind reeled. This is mass hysteria! "No," I argued, "it's so peaceful, so tranquil. So right, somehow."

My pew must be plugged into an electrical outlet, my logic argued. I've had shocks from many of Darko's washing machines — this was similar.

Now we were standing. 'We Lift Up Holy Hands in Thy Name, We Lift Them Up Lord, Unto Thy Name'. . . Electricity started shooting through my body in two inch skips. Up and down. Down to my toes and back up to my head. I was on fire. I thought I was going to light up. But, I'm not sitting on a pew, so, how did they do that? I felt a very cool hand move across the back of my neck under my hair. I turned to see if the people behind me were touching me. To my amazement, their eyes closed, arms in the air, their faces tender and intent, they were oblivious to my very presence. That's when I noticed it. Something I had never seen before in my life. I had NEVER seen ANYONE worshipping God. They were sincere. I could see it on their faces. This was genuine.

Finally, we sat down. Was I frightened, I wondered, by all of this? No, it wasn't at all spooky or eerie. It was genuine love. I could feel it... reach out and actually touch it.

The service ended. "Mom, we have to come back here next Sunday," Dan burst out. I turned, surprised that a boy, almost eleven, but going on fifteen, would get excited about coming back to a church next week.

"Did you feel anything, Dan?" I asked timidly.

"Yes" Stevie interrupted, "Oh, yes, mommy — I felt GOD in HERE!"

Of course he did. He was sitting on the same pew as me. People were now shaking my hand, asking if I enjoyed the service. They must realize I'm new. No, it didn't seem that way. They didn't seem to be doing it out of duty or something expected of them. Their eyes showed they really were interested, that they really cared.

"Dan, Steve, we're going to come back just one more time. I have to find out just what's happening in there."

Next day I went to see the priest, who gave me permission to attend. I didn't know him and he didn't know me. I told him detail by detail, what had happened the previous night and asked if I could go back next week.

"Of course, of course. Praise God. But, don't stay there. Come back and show us, teach us, we're just starting a Charismatic movement. We don't really know what we're doing yet." He went on and on about the Holy Spirit. I didn't have a clue what he was talking about and, I was in a hurry — had to see my lawyer about the bankruptcy.

"Donna, isn't there some way you can catch up on the payments?" Don asked. "It's no use, Don. How does one pay off more than $200,000? We can't begin to earn that much."

"Donna, your problem is that other house. That's almost a thousand dollars a month you're losing. Sell it for less, give it away; anything."

"We can't sell it for much less, when it's mortgaged to the hilt. What about the income tax? I'd still owe them. I'd have to get enough to pay the first mortgage, the second, and the twelve thousand in back taxes."

Then a thought struck me. The one thing, since I bought the Bible that stood out, as if jumping out of the pages, was Malachi 3:10: 'Bring ye all the tithes into the storehouse, that there may be meat in mine house and prove me now herewith, sayeth the Lord of host, if I will not open you the windows of heaven and pour you out a blessing, that there shall not be room enough to receive it."

"Prove me," God said. "PROVE ME." The only verse in the Bible which God challenges us to PROVE He's there.

"Don, postpone the bankruptcy for about a week; maybe ten days. I have an idea."

"Gladly. I don't want to see you go under, not after the fight you've put up."

It wasn't my idea, it was God's — PROVE ME. Okay, I thought, if you're up there, for sure, I'm going to prove you, next Sunday. Somehow, somewhere I'm going to get fifteen dollars for the collection plate.

When I told Darko, he flipped out.

"Fifteen dollars to a CHURCH? HAVE YOU GONE MAD? Where are you going to get fifteen dollars?"

"I don't know. I always find the money for cigarettes. I'll find it, now, for this. I'll sell the toaster; I don't know, but I am going to 'prove God', Darko. He says He's going to bless us.

Darko knew I would anyway, whether he objected or not.

All week I watched broadcasts on Christian TV. I used to flick the channels and think they were square and corny, but now I was hearing things similar to what I heard Sunday night. They were saying the same thing, praying the same way. They talked about God and the love of Jesus. I had pictured God as someone sitting on a cloud just waiting to ZAP me every time I stepped out of line. I hadn't wanted much to do with Him. If He was keeping track of all the Sundays I had missed, not going to church, I was really in trouble.

They talked of God's mercy. He loved me so much He came and died in my place, so I could inherit eternal life. It wasn't His will "that one should perish, but that all should come to repentance". (2 Peter 3:9)

WOW! I'd never heard this before. I couldn't wait for Sunday morning. But let's be practical about this. Don't let anyone pull anything over on you. This all sounds good, but is it real?

Sunday, February 17th, 1980

Sue wanted to sit close to the front. Too close, I thought. I couldn't survey the whole church from this close.

Reynold Rutledge, a baritone I had seen and heard just the previous week on a Christian TV program, called 100 Huntley Street, sang the following song, which I found affected me profoundly:

Unworthy am I of the grace that He gave
Unworthy to hold to His hand
Amazed that a King would reach down to us man
This mercy, I cannot understand

Unworthy, unworthy, a beggar in bondage, alone
But He made me worthy
And now by His grace
His mercy has made me His own

Unworthy am I of the glory to come
Unworthy with angels to sing
I thrill just to know that He loved me so much
A pauper, I walk with a king

That about said it. Unworthy to walk with the KING. Three men were sitting at the altar. All wearing suits. Two of them were the pastors of the church. The third was Rev. Keith Parks, who was on his way to Iceland from B.C. and had stopped, en route. I soon realized that he had never been at this church. He didn't know I was new here, either. The other two might notice I was not a regular, but he wouldn't.

His eyes kept meeting mine. I tried to look very nonchalant, yet when he started his message, I knew beyond a shadow of a doubt, he was talking to me. He knew me and my present dilemma.

They're mind readers. They had to be. Think quick. Do mathematical equations in your head. (This was my greatest talent. I'd never used a calculator. I could multiply double digits in my head.) Throw him off. It didn't work. He must be picking my subconscious. But I knew what he was saying. I kept glancing away; looking disinterested.

"God has laid something upon my heart for this day. God has victory in mind for you. I'm thinking of the troubles and problems in your life and the future victory in your life. In the midst of crisis, problems and the battles of life, in your life, when there seems to be no answer, and you don't know what to do -- God always provides a man to do the job for an impossible task."

(Did I have a crisis, a problem, a battle, no apparent answer? You bet I did!)

"God provides the tool to do the job. It won't be the tool the world thinks should be used. Take the tool. . . God will fight your battle. It's not what we do and we think that will win the battle. . . so many give up, because they give up when it gets tough.

They shall know that the Lord saves! The battle is not our own. It is the Lord's. It's in the midst of the battle, we see that God helps us. Wouldn't it be nice if there were no car accidents, no financial problems, no crisis? He has the ultimate answer and solution, so He can bring you to victory. Don't despise the battle. The battle is the Lord's.

"God provides the will to go through it. The will to know God will help him because he had some experiences in the past, when God's will and your will have meshed. God provides the Victory to your life. Don't worry about the battles, rejoice in victory.

a) God has provided a man for your battle . . . Jesus Christ. The ONLY man.

b) God provides the tool. . . the cross is God's tool. Jesus Christ died for the sins of the world to bring mankind to Himself.

c) God provides the means . . . through the blood of Jesus Christ, we are justified. It was always the shedding of innocent blood which redeemed mankind, by the remission of sin.

d) God provides the battle. . . taking your sin and my sin upon Himself. The Son of God.

e) God provides the will. . . Jesus Christ did the will of the Father to die in man's place and gave Him the will to do it.

f) God provided the Victory. Any problem you have, Christ has already fought it for you.

"You can have the victory by coming to Jesus Christ. Whosoever is born of God overcometh the world, overcome the battle. YOU'RE THE PERSON!

"He'll provide the tool, maybe a TV evangelist. He'll provide the means. The Holy Spirit hits the mark every time. He will guide.

"So many think they carry the battles of the world. But the battles make you or break you. Satan is trying to divide and break your home. Satan fighting God. But God provides the VICTORY as Satan versus God.

"God is speaking to you through the Holy Spirit. I can see the agony in your eyes. Beloved, the battle is not yours. The Holy Spirit is saying, 'Come to Jesus Christ and He'll take you through this process of life and bring ultimate victory to you'.

Can you say, 'I came to this church today to give my battle to Jesus Christ?' Will you say, 'Come into my life Lord Jesus. I'll lay the battle at your feet.' Jesus Christ is your answer. Not your own stubborn will.

I'm waiting for a lady this morning. God's speaking to you. One especially. I don't want to point you out, the Holy Spirit has already pointed you out. That struggle in your home. That wife and husband brought to the last straw. God loves you and cares for you. He's the only one that can help you. A family, a mother, raise your hand. That hand represents a life, a woman that you're calling. Let the man Jesus bring a healing to their home and to their life and give them a victorious future. And their loved ones that are not here this morning save them also. Family members many miles away don't even know prayers have been answered here today. Bow your heads in prayer."

I was relieved. No shocks, no cold hands, just relief.

"You have to claim your miracle." he continued. "Raise your hand." No way! I quickly slipped my fingertips under each buttock, just in case my arms shot up by themselves in this place. You never could tell.

"The Holy Spirit pointed you out to me when I entered the sanctuary." Holy Spirit? I glanced up without lifting my head.

He WAS looking directly at ME. It couldn't be. Go away, my mind screamed.

"There's a lady sitting directly in front of me. PLEASE receive your miracle."

I glanced up again. Whew, there were two women in the pew in front of me. It's my imagination, he must mean one of them. I glanced over my shoulder. Twenty to thirty people had their hands up. Why are you picking on me? Look at all the people responding. Why me?

His voice grew severe — "If you don't put your hand up, I'm coming down and pointing you out." My head shot up. He was POINTING AT ME, with his index finger. My hand shot up, my head snapped back down.

"Thank you, thank you. I knew it was you." he sighed.

Thank God it's over, I thought. No — not quite — now he was saying, "Those who had their hands up join me at the front of the altar."

Looking directly at him, I shook my head from side to side, "No way. I'm not. No way." — and at that moment I was just lifted. Not on my own power; more like angels were lifting me by the shoulders and carrying me, a few inches off the floor, to the altar. I was numb from the shoulders down. I was not controlling my legs.

He bypassed all the others, came around to where I stood and, placing his arm around my shoulders, said tenderly, "You've received your miracle. It's over. You belong to Christ."

"I don't want a miracle." I was crying, black tears streamed down my face. There was a lady in a wheelchair beside me. "She needs the miracle. I just want to live without the devil at my heels."
"I know. You've had a dreadful couple of years. It's over. It's over. I don't understand why she doesn't receive her's. Maybe you need your miracle more right now."

I was sobbing.

Black tears stained my dress.

I gathered the kids and zoomed home. Anxiously, I waited for Darko. Would he believe all this? Never! I don't even believe it myself. I want it, but I don't believe it.

He came through the door asking, "Were you in church today?"

"Yes, wait till you hear what happened." I exclaimed excited.

"Whatever happened, here's forty bucks for next Sunday."

"What? Why? What happened?", I wondered, forgetting my miracle. This in itself was a miracle. Darko offering money to a CHURCH! The only thing that would have surprised me more was if my father offered money to a church. 'All crooks,' he'd said many times.

"I earned $400.00 today."

"Where?"

"Selling antiques. It happened about 1:00 p.m. It was unbelievable, the junk that I sold."

It was unbelievable. He had gone three Sundays in a row and didn't make the twenty dollars to cover the cost of the booth. "Whatever it is," he continued, "the power of positive thinking, or whatever, I don't know, but it works."

I proceeded to tell him about Keith Parks. Would he come back with me to the six o'clock service? "No, take your mother. I'll play cards with your dad."

"M-O-T-H-E-R" I was racing up the stairs . . . "Wait till you Hear!" I told the whole story from A - Z, "What do you think?"

She cried. Naturally.

"But will you go with me? Tonight?"

"Sure Donna, okay." Her eyes wide now with astonishment, wondering why I kept running into GOD.

That evening, driving up. . . "It says temple on it. Donna, it's JEWISH."

"It's not, mother, it's nondenominational."

"You've brought me to a Jewish temple."

"I don't know why it says temple. Stop it — it's not Jewish, it's Christian."

"Where are the statues?" We were now inside the sanctuary.

"Be quiet. I don't know."

"There's no crucifix, Donna."

"There was a cross outside. Didn't you see the cross? Be quiet."

"Which one's the priest? Why isn't he dressed?"

"They're both pastors. They wear suits."

"Oh my goodness, one's got a beard!"

"Jesus had a beard. So what? Are you going to keep quiet? Please, SHUT UP."

Nothing supernatural happened. The music was extraordinary though. My kind of music.

'Father God, we give all thanks and praise to Thee,
Father God, our hands we humbly raise to Thee,
For Thy love and Thy mighty power amazes me, amazes me,
As I stand in awe and worship Father God.'

I didn't light up. I was disappointed. My mother didn't light up. It was difficult keeping her quiet, but — nothing. After the service ended, I walked up to Rev. Parks and introduced my mother.

"We're all going to be praying for Donna," he said. Then turning to my mother, he asked, "Would you like prayer for yourself?"

My mother, the one who couldn't care less whether she had twenty-five cents or twenty-five million in her purse, made the following statement: "I just don't want to fight with my Nick over quarters anymore." I almost fell over. I'll never forget that statement as long as I live. This couldn't come out of my mother's lips. You would have to know her to understand. If she had said, "Donna's too skinny," or "the boy are too skinny, they should eat more"; that wouldn't surprise me, but MONEY?! My mother mentioning money???

All the way home she nagged. "Nothing spectacular! No miracle! No cruicifix! Go to a Catholic mass!"

"Mother, you haven't been in a church in six years, since Stevie was christened. YOU go to a Catholic mass, I'm coming here."

All that next week, after I'd postponed the bankruptcy, I soaked up the Bible. Couldn't put it down. I was like a magnet. "The Infallible Word of God," they'd called it. Why? I'd have to check this out; against history, against science, against evolution. This is either the instruction manual of God or the biggest fairy tale anyone ever wrote.

I prayed fervently every night, "In the name of Jesus". I'd learned this was important, even crucial. He was the mediator between God and man, the High Priest seated at the right hand of God, making intercession for us. There was no other way God would hear our prayers, unless we came to Him through the sacrifice of His Son, the innocent sacrifice which bridged us to God Almighty. Without His sacrificial death, we were alienated from God because of our sin nature.

HEAVY STUFF! I just soaked it in, but at the same time I was reading everything else I could lay my hands on to disprove it. The boys and I would join in one of the bedrooms and pray timidly, awkwardly. Not an easy task to put into practice so quickly. Stevie now wanted to add to my ". . . and watch over and protect us tomorrow, dear Lord," "And forgive grampa for swearing so much. He really doesn't mean it. Amen."

This happened at 9:15 p.m. The following morning my mother was jabbering on the phone, "We won!!! WE WON $25,000 on the lottery last night! Donna, come quick. WE WON!" (The lottery draw was from 9:00 to 9:30 on Thursday evenings.)

I should have learned never to ask, but. . . "Dad, if you could lend me $1,500 I wouldn't have to go bankrupt. Would you?"

He'd always say, 'You'll go further into the hole until you won't be able to get out any more."

"Take a chance on me, Dad. Even if we do go bankrupt, I'll pay you back. I know I will."

"I offered to lend you three thousand before and you said it wouldn't help. Nothing short of $100,000 would help. Now you tell me fifteen hundred dollars will halt the bankruptcy."

"I know, but I didn't believe in miracles then. All I have to do is sell that other house and pay off the tax man and I'll be home free!"

He agreed!

My dad had tears in his eyes. "I know this fell from heaven, Donna. I'm not lucky. I've had to work and slave for every nickel. I know this is a miracle."

"You just have to give 10% to charity. You HAVE TO! You'll never lack anything again. Ever. It's a promise, from the Bible." I should not have said that.

"I'll give $250 to the Croatian church, but, no way $2,500. No way! That's too much, they don't need it as badly as I do. I'm getting old."

"Don't bother. If it's not 10%, it won't be blessed. One percent is not a tithe, it's only tipping God. Don't you understand, the more you give, the more you receive? The Bible says, 'He which soweth sparingly shall reap also sparingly; and he which soweth bountifully shall reap also bountifully! It works. I can't wait to see how much I'm going to give next week."

I'm happy to say, I never looked back.

I cried all over city hall about the damage to my expropriated property. "What is it you want, Mrs. Martonfi? The city paid your legal fees in the expropriation case."

I replied, "$12,500.00. Another $12,500 would make it fair."

Next morning, my cheque was ready, and the tax man paid off! (I cried all over his office too, and he allowed me the extra time needed, when he realized he couldn't get a plugged nickel.) I signed papers saying I released the city from any further compensation.

Twice, every Sunday, I went to church. If I worked late on a real estate offer the Saturday before and couldn't get out of bed, Darko was pulling me by my feet. "You have to go to church. Things are different since you've been going. Get up, you're going to be late."

Pulling the covers over my head I'd mutter, "You go then, I'm tired. Let me sleep."
He wouldn't. Neither would the boys. "Mom, we want to go to church!"
Without God pulling at the heart strings, would it be natural for three boys to want to spend Sunday in church? This was a switch! God didn't consider it a catastrophe if I missed church, but now my family did!

I also should have learned to get some waterproof mascara. I had never been a crier, except in serious catastrophes, such as at the tax department and at city hall. But each week I'd strive my best not to cry, and I just poured like a faucet. It wasn't because of sadness or hardship; they were tears of joy, relief and an outpouring of love.

"Let this be real," I cried one night. "Please God, let it be real. I need you. Don't let me wake up one morning to find it gone. Be real, PLEASE!"

I had never been with 300 people that radiated so much love, concern, care and warmth.

One day, I happened to mention to some church ladies that I was having problems with Stevie on Sundays. He was usually so well behaved anywhere else I took him. He fidgeted so much, fell asleep on my lap, got diarrhea, or turned hot with fever, each and every service. There was always something to distract me. It was very unusual.

"I left him home today and he cried, because he couldn't go."

Right there and then, in the middle of the restaurant, they offered to pray. We joined hands even. I expected that people would stare and gawk, but everyone around seemed as touched as I was.

"Lord, we offer this problem to you. We ask that you place your loving arms around Steven during the service and keep him from the evil one. We dedicate this child to you, Lord. In Jesus' name we pray. Amen."

They were real. I was speechless. To think someone would not be ashamed to pray out loud, in a crowded restaurant, over a little tiny problem of mine. I must add, he has never batted an eye since; no stomach aches, no falling asleep, a perfect little angel.

One Sunday while we were all standing, the pastor asked anyone who had not been baptized by the Holy Spirit, to sit down. Had I been? I'd lit up many times, but baptized as on the day of Pentecost, when the Holy Spirit came to the apostles and other Christians? I didn't know. As if Pastor Fred knew my thoughts, he said, "Even if you're not sure, be seated."

I sat down. Two dear ladies came and sat beside me, Marion and Jenny. They started to pray. They were praying in tongues, the universal language of God and the angels. I didn't know just anyone could pray like that. I thought it was a gift to merely a few. It sounded like Hebrew.

"Pray out loud," Jenny encouraged. I bowed my head only to have it then shoot back, raised to heaven and my vocal cords started vibrating at what seemed to be one million vibrations per minute. You couldn't duplicate the physical experience if you tried. A language proceeded from my lips, a language I had not learned. It flowed. Flowed like living water. Words flowing out, streams of water, seemingly, flowing in, simultaneously. It was Acts 19:6: 'And when Paul had laid his hands upon them, the Holy Ghost came on them; and they spake with tongues, and prophesied'.

"Daddy, Daddy, Mommy spoke in another language. You should have been there. Do it again, Mom."

Darko raised his eyebrows. "I think I'd better come and see what kind of church you've been going to."

"You mean it? You'll come?" I knew if I could just get him to come, he'd meet with God eventually. I knew it. For some reason I knew that was what I had prayed in the heavenly language; the language of God. The Holy Spirit interceding to the Father, on my husband's behalf.

'And in the same way, by our faith, the Holy Spirit helps us with our daily problems and in our praying. For we don't even know what we should pray for, nor how to pray as we should; but the Holy Spirit prays for us with such feeling that it cannot be expressed in words. 'And the Father who knows all hearts knows, of course, what the Spirit is saying as He pleads for us in harmony with God's own will.' (Romans 8:26, 27 TLB).

The following Sunday morning, Darko came to church. Again, nothing spectacular. The choir and the guest soloist were exceptional; but no sparks.

'I can feel the touch of angel's wings I see glory on each face, Surely the presence of the Lord is in this place.'

That song alone could help me reach heaven and His presence. His presence, yes; but Darko needed to be zapped. Nothing short of zapped would do. He had dozens of arguments against God. An actual supernatural creator? Well, he wouldn't believe it till he saw Him, face to face.

Many greeted and introduced themselves to us. I dubiously watched for his reaction.

"The entertainment's worth the price of admission. Better than I've seen at the O'Keefe Centre. These people are different, somehow. I can't put my finger on it, but there's something special about them."

"Are you going to come back?"

"W-e-l-l, not every Sunday, but sure, I'll come again."

Hallelujah. Praise the Lord. Darko going to church. He had passed the point of saying, "If there is a God, He gave me two arms, two legs and a mind. I choose my own destiny, my own fate."

We didn't have a destiny and our fate looked bleak. "I don't care, Donna," he used to say, "you'll have to prove to me that the universe wasn't started by two sparks."

Hold on Darko — I won't have to, Jesus Christ will. HOLD ON TO YOUR SEAT!

Chapter Eight

NOW YOU'RE GONNA SEE MIRACLES!

The more books I read, which was now one every other night, the more facts I was uncovering to prove the Bible. I could not understand why the media didn't carry these accounts; why they weren't taught in schools. The more advanced we became, the more we proved what the prophets had known thousands of years prior. What they wrote then, our doctors and scientists were just uncovering now, in the nineteenth and twentieth centuries. You had to dig, and dig hard for the information. If the news and media covered these facts, people all over the world would be flocking and standing in line to get a copy of the Bible.

I couldn't possibly relate all the information I have uncovered in the dozens of books that I have read, but just to give an example, I will briefly outline some facts that have amazed me personally. Not until the early nineteen hundreds did we know the following:

—that the blood of animals is different from humans

—the blood of all races is the same

—the blood of a dead person is lethal

—the skin is first formed on the embryo, not the bones

—the components which make up our skin and bones are the identical components which are found in earth (God created man from earth)

—I believe even the first anesthesia was performed by God when He put Adam into a 'deep' sleep and removed his rib.

Another fact which I found fascinating was regarding our lunar landing. When we landed on the moon, only a fraction of an inch of dust was found to be covering the surface. If the moon was as old as science had been saying for years, then the astronauts would have sunk many feet into the dust. The fact that there was less than an inch, and considering the hundreds of thousands of tons of dust that fall on the moon annually, attracted by its gravitational pull, this only proves that it can't be more than about ten thousand years old. The moon could not have possibly been rotating around the earth for even a couple of hundred thousand years, much less millions.

I was so overjoyed by the new found power I had received from the Holy Spirit, and all the biblical promises that went with it, that I decided to try it out after Darko had been very sick for three days with a bad flu. The following evening was the big real estate banquet which I desperately wanted to attend. Darko had a high fever with chills and all the frills. Pus was running out both of his eyes. I waited till he was asleep, and not really knowing what I was doing, started reading all the 'healing' passages, claiming the healing power of Jesus, through His stripes.

It actually worked! When he woke in the morning, you would not have known he had been ill in bed for days. There was not one sign or trace of the flu.

"It worked. It worked! The Lord healed you!"

"What are you talking about?"

"While you were sleeping, I prayed and claimed healing from the Lord for you. He healed you."

"Don't be ridiculous. Any flu has to run its course. I'd be better even if you hadn't prayed."
We went to the banquet, but the next morning Darko was sicker than he had been previously.

"Pray again."

"No. It doesn't work that way. You didn't give the glory to God. You first have to believe, then pray yourself. The healing is there, but you have to believe and know it is there to get it. It's like if someone put a million dollars in a bank account for you. Unless you believe it's there, and go to make a withdrawal, you could be so poor you could starve to death. It doesn't do any good just being there or having it, you have to know the account number and how to take it out."

In the weeks that followed, I heard many testimonies about the miraculous healings people had received. Tumors the size of half a football had disintegrated. Paralysis was cured. One testimony in particular affected me. A young man, who had suffered since birth with epilepsy, which was always preceded by a migraine headache; was healed.

I had suffered with migraines from the time I was twelve. My whole left side would go tingly, including my nose and mouth and I would have what I called "white outs". There were large blank patches of white in front of my eyes. My vocal cords would paralyze, preventing me from speaking and I would suffer excruciating pain for hours.

This fellow went on to say, that once he became saved, at the onset of the migraine, he pointed his finger at his temple and said, "Satan, in the name of Jesus, I rebuke this attack." The headache subsided and was not followed by an epileptic seizure. The next day, when he would feel the headache approaching, he pointed to his head and said, "Satan, in the name of Jesus. . ." without finishing the sentence, he could feel immediate relief. The following day, the pain hit quickly and without warning. This time all he had to do was point to his head and immediately the pain vanished, as quickly as it had started.

"You do not have to accept anything from Satan. Rebuke him in the precious name of Jesus. Seven years have passed since that experience, and I praise God that I have not had even a normal headache, nor an epileptic seizure since."

I knew, there and then, that I would never again have a migraine headache. I never have.

About the third time Darko had come to church, merely four months after I had my 'miracle service', the service again wasn't spectacular. Good, but not spectacular. Once again, there was a visiting evangelist and he was speaking about the baptism of the Holy Spirit. By the end of the service, Darko was sobbing. He was shaking, with tears just streaming down his face. I was ecstatic. Pastor George acknowledged the huge smile on my face. Praise God! Darko got zapped. He'd never doubt that there was a God again. It took him quite a while to compose himself.

"I came into contact with God. He took this great big, huge, soft fist and hit me square between the eyes. It's fantastic. I've met God! Donna, He's there. He's real. I don't believe it. There is a God! I've actually met the Living God."

We discussed it all day. All the experiences I had come home telling him about, he now understood. He had questions. Millions of questions. He was hungry for more. You don't just run into God and then go about your business and ignore Him. Things happen. You change.

When I became saved, or 'born again', I wanted to drag the whole world to church with me. I wanted everyone to experience what I did. I told everyone I knew, plus a few strangers, that the Lord could step into their lives and give them unimaginable joy and fulfillment.

It was all taken with a grain of salt, because this was 'Donna -- She BELIEVED in miracles. She was always 'high'. She lived her life exuberantly and any little thing could wind her up and make her glow'... But when Darko now confirmed everything I had said as gospel and would proclaim, "You'd better listen, this is for real," people listened with a different attitude. Here was this great big hulk, whom you could never budge, under any circumstances, always cool and calm. . . PREACHING!

His mother would say, "This is all nonsense. You're completely crazy. Dana, the day Darko talks with God or God talks to him, then I'll believe it."

Now her son was coming to her with the same message: "God answers prayer. You must be 'born again' You have to believe in Jesus Christ to enter the kingdom of God. He's alive!"

We thought she would respond immediately. "You said if I ever met God, you'd believe it. Well I did, and I regret each and every day of my life that I've lived without that knowledge."

"You're crazy too. They hypnotized you. You can't go around talking like this. Everyone believes Jesus Christ lived two thousand years ago and was crucified. So what? But to say He communicates with people is stupid. They've hypnotized you, so they can get your money."

"Why then do you go to fortune tellers and communicate with ghosts and the dead?" I couldn't help pushing at this point.

"I don't really believe that. I go just in case. I believe when you die, your spirit goes to another world. Who knows, maybe it wanders around and can communicate with witches."

"If you believe that maybe ghosts can communicate with witches, then why do you think it's stupid to believe that Jesus Christ, who is God, can't communicate with us, especially when you're instructed in the Holy Word of God, the Bible, that He has been, ever since the beginning of time?"

"He hasn't. I don't believe that."

She agreed to come to our church though. We prayed that the Lord would reach out and touch her. We knew He'd only have the one chance. She'd never come again if He didn't make Himself real to her.

When she started to cry after the service, my heart leaped. But the tears were not for the reason I'd hoped. "It upset me when I saw that woman and her daughter hugging at the altar and I think of the horrible things my daughter says and does to me. Never a kind word. It breaks my heart. You're the cause of that, Dana. Until we came to Canada we were a lovely family. She turned wild at fifteen, just when we met you. Ran away from home and went on dope. She spit on me and kicked me. Coming home drunk at that age:; I have you to thank."

I hardly ever saw Maria in the three years I dated Darko. She'd just pop her head in for 'hello' or 'good-bye' and that's all we ever saw of her till years later when we married.

I was brought up very strictly. I was quite a decent teenager. My dad was so strict he didn't even let me stay out late the night of my graduation, although I had already been engaged for over a year. I was always expected home by midnight, up until the day I got married. If I had ever stayed away from home for three or four days, my dad would have broken me in two with his bare hands. Just smoking cigarettes in those days was considered DARING. Nobody tried dope.

I had just come to an important realization; I realized her words didn't hurt, didn't bother me, didn't raise my blood pressure. It was as if she was attacking someone else, instead of me. There was no dislike for her, no hate. I figured she had to blame someone for her daughter going wild, so it might as well be me.

I also realized that this was not my own nature responding; it was the Lord's. It was His Spirit. My feathers would have been more than ruffled by this accusation, but instead I was filled with kindness and sympathy. Time and again, He's proved that He has given us a new spirit and made us a new creature; "Therefore if any man be in Christ, he is a new creature; old things are passed away; behold, all things are become new.' (2 Corinthians 5:17)

I had noticed this change of heart from the very first day. Only days after my 'miracle service' my taste in TV shows changed dramatically. I never watched more than three programs a week anyway, but they were programs I would schedule my life around, not to miss. Now I was appalled by the garbage I had been watching for years. I developed a distaste for my favorite shows and actually loathed the lifestyle they represented. I weighed every word in a new light. I couldn't find one show which appealed to me or held my attention except for the Christian broadcasts.

Stranger than my new awareness of the junk on TV, was the realization that I had lost all my fear. I no longer had claustrophobia. I no longer feared dogs, and had challenged that many a time with the largest of breeds. Dogs, instead of searching me out, completely ignored me. I did not spook, ever. The evil presence I once felt, was replaced by a peace, "a peace that passed all understanding." A peace that I was a child of God. When you know who walks with you and whose you are, nothing can scare you. Not even death, for to die means to be immediately in the presence of Christ. I had been reared, as have many, to believe we have to spend time in purgatory, paying for the sins which we have committed. No wonder death is so horrendous, to so many, and people sometimes shriek in fear on their death beds. No one told them that Jesus paid the ultimate price for their sins, on His cross. No one could render that payment. No one needs to. When He was on the cross and the thief hanging beside Him asked to be remembered, He answered, 'this day thou shalt be with me in paradise'. To leave this world is to be immediately in the presence of the Lord, if you have believed in Him. What or whom then can you ever fear here on earth, being just a heartbeat from Him? Death is just a step from the visible into the invisible. . . and eternity.

2 Timothy 1:7 says "For God hath not given us the spirit of fear; but of power, and of love, and of a sound mind."

I also quickly learned the dangers of the occult. How the Lord warns against dabbling with any form of the supernatural:

Astrology, Ouija Boards, fortune tellers, etc. You don't have to go to a Satanic mass to summon the devil. He's real and he comes quickly to those who think they are just having fun with it.

"I don't really believe in it. I'm just playing with it. I don't take it seriously" they'd say. How do you play with Satan? How do you not take him seriously? He's very intelligent and has had thousands and thousands of years' of experience at camouflaging and disguising his road to death and darkness as fun and games. I think his greatest triumph was when people started to think of him in a little red suit with horns and a pitch fork. Who could possible take that seriously? They forget he was the most beautiful and intelligent being that God created.

If you believe in God, then you must believe everything He has ever said, such as "We are not battling with flesh and blood but against principalities, against powers, against the rulers of the darkness of this world, against spiritual wickedness in high places".

He warns us over and over to take it VERY seriously and renounce any involvement in it whatsoever, to get rid of and destroy any zodiac signs, tarot cards or anything associated with magic. It is all black magic, there is no white magic. If you're going to go looking for the devil, God will not interfere, but will allow you to suffer the consequences of what you have pursued, even if you're doing it for fun. But there is nothing 'fun' about Satan. He's called 'The Destroyer'.

We had to do such a housecleaning. It was amazing how many zodiac signs, pendants and carved Buddhas we had accumulated. Rabbits' feet, horse shoes and books on astrology, all went into the trash. I wasn't going to give the devil even one small foothold.

The Lord is strict about His people not having any association with the "ruler of this world". Fortune tellers would promise you the "glorious, prosperous future" you had come seeking, but instead the more you chase the supernatural, the worse your destiny and the worse your outcome. Just watch people, and there are many, 'just having fun' with these things and see how their marriages deteriorate, their kids start running amuck, financial pressures increase, jobs and careers go sour. I personally have seen it happen to dozens. The worse life gets for them, the deeper they get involved, seeking answers and solutions. All ending up unhappy, discouraged or on drugs and alcohol; not one living a normal, stable existence but plagued by catastrophe after catastrophe. Statistics show that divorced people are the unhappiest of all groups of individuals, yet it looked like the easy way out, back to the single set and freedom.

God ordained the family and marriage. Satan is the one out to destroy and divide the family unit. Is it a wonder that they're unhappy?

Jesus came so that we could have life, and have it more abundantly. (John 10:10) Satan and his religion came "to steal, and to kill, and to destroy", with disease, poverty, stress and immorality.

Many times I have been asked, "if there is a God, why does He make wars and famines and hardship?" He DOESN'T. He gave man the Garden of Eden. Man blew it — not God, but God gets blamed. Man made the choice to obey the evil one, instead of God. All Satan had to do was lie to Eve and then confuse her as far as what it was that God had commanded; and this planet and its' inhabitants fell from grace. Just look at the countries that are starving and hungry. They're worshipping false gods. They're pursuing Allah, Buddha, Hinduism, Transcendental Meditation, Yoga, Reincarnation and Spiritism, and God Almighty gets the blame for their misfortunes.

In the past few decades, people of North America, including government leaders, are reading their horoscope charts daily and seeking after psychics and mystics for the answers for their lives. Every sixty minutes, a teenager commits suicide and 12% of the school kids are using drugs. All the filth of the world is pumped into these teens by the entertainment industries, but they're not allowed to pray in our public schools. Someone's afraid they might get a bit of God in them ... but they wonder why God has forsaken them. Look who turned his back. It wasn't God!... but, no one needs to stay forsaken. "He that believeth on the Son hath everlasting life; and he that believeth not the Son shall not see life; but the wrath of God abideth on him." (John 3:36).

The decision is yours. It's either black or white, God or Satan. There is no gray in this life. That's not the Master's plan. You shall either serve "God or Mammon".

My parent's eyes just widened, hearing Darko confirm this knowledge and understanding of God. They never suspected he could be influenced by anything, much less so strongly and adamantly profess that he had a personal relationship now with the Almighty. So, now they worked on the kids.

"That church is bad. It's brainwashing you. They're going to kidnap you and take you to some far off country. They want all your money. Don't go there anymore."

Unfortunately, the Jim Jones caper had just previously come to a head with the murder and suicide of nearly one thousand people. Jim Jones was an atheist and had set himself up as God, demanding that his followers worship him.

My children had may times heard stories how I was frightened into being good. How I was told there were boogie men in the basement and attic, just waiting to pounce on me the moment I misbehaved. How I was told that all the people walking the streets were gypsies who were looking for children that they could grab and then pull out their eyes and make soap out of them. When I would lose the key to our house, I would crawl into a hole under the veranda. I laid there sometimes till 7:30 at night, till my parents came home, my heart in my throat, listening to the footsteps going up and down the street; feeling terrified.

They weren't buying this scare tactic. They'd been raised not to blindly believe anything but to judge for themselves. Not to be frightened into other people's opinions, but to make up their own minds. It didn't matter what gramma said. Now out-numbered, gramma again agreed to come to church; at least to hear Pastor George sing.

"He sings better than Humperdink" she'd say. "Why doesn't he go into show business? It's such a waste of talent singing in a church."

"He left show business to become a pastor, mother."

The Spirit of God was evident and moving. The service was beautiful. "They're all wearing mink. They buy mink coats with the collection money."

"I just can't understand why everyone is crying?" she's now relating to my dad, "That is so stupid. All those people crying. What's there to cry about?"

"Mother, when you can cry for someone else, someone else's pain, rather than just your own, then maybe you'll be happy. I can't believe you weren't moved or touched by that service. You witnessed a miracle and it went right over your head. You were in the presence of God and you were counting mink coats."

"Miracle? What miracle? What happened?" she looked amazed, wondering what she had missed.

It was true; Jesus said, "Whosoever shall seek me with all his heart shall find me", and "Behold, I stand at the door and knock; if any man hear my voice, and open the door, I will come in to him and will sup with him, and he with me." Jesus makes Himself available to 'whosoever' but you can't shut your heart, slam the door, be completely close-minded, and still expect Him to show Himself to you. He's not a gate crasher. He waits to be invited. He did not create robots. He gave us our free will so that we would gladly and willingly seek His face of our own accord.

Right from the beginning, I had said that I would draw the line at being re-baptized. I'd keep my 'in' as a Catholic, just in case. Darko felt the same.

"Oh, I couldn't get baptized and get in that tank at my age." Within months, the Lord had changed our hearts. He drew us so strongly that we couldn't wait for the next baptismal service.

My parents went hysterical. "I won't allow you to re-christen yourself. Don't you dare. What will our relatives say? We'll be the talk of the town. No Catholic has ever renounced the faith of his birth and his mother. If you re-christen the kids, I'll never forgive you. I'll renounce you." My dad was throwing tantrums.

"How can you do this, Donna? What's the matter with you?" my mother wailed. "I won't hear of it. Never! You wouldn't dare." Now she was really crying.

"It wasn't my decision, it's what the Lord wants. He keeps asking and drawing me to be baptized. Jesus' mother didn't sprinkle water on him when he was a baby. He was a grown man when He made the decision and was immersed in water. For us this signifies our old selves going into the grave with Him. I follow only His Instructions and no one else's; not any church's, not any priest's or pastor's. I do what He leads me to do."

"You can't tell me God told you to be baptized. He wouldn't tell you such a thing."

"He did, mother, and I'm not going to argue with Him or with you. It's final. I'd like for you to be there. I also wish you'd read the Bible and then maybe you'd know what He wants us to do and what He says."

Unbelievably, when we set a date with the pastors, we found that Keith Parks was going to be there that same service.

That was more than special. I found that God was constantly throwing in these special little blessings. The 'Big Whoppers' I somehow understood: Darko got a good job; I was selling houses and the deals were all closing; the other house was rented and the mortgage took care of itself; the income tax was paid; no misfortunes, every day was brighter than the day before; but it was these little extras that meant so much. He cared so much about these little things.

The man, to whom the Holy Spirit had pointed me out, when I was desperate and thoroughly in the dark, would witness the 'victory'. Of all the weekends to pop back! It only confirmed how special this day was to the Lord, because someone was obedient to His will.

The only relatives that I dearly and truly loved — Uncle Tom, Aunt Vera and Vera's mother Maka — were coming from Windsor for the long weekend. I especially loved Maka. She was a dear, sweet, elderly lady, with the disposition of an angel and a face to match.

Uncle Tom noticed it first. "Donna, you seem so calm, so at peace. There's something different about you."

"Yes," said Vera, "it's a kind of peaceful radiance."

"I've found Jesus Christ." I replied.

"Oh, don't start that again. You and that stupid church." My dad hollered and quickly changed the subject.

Maka was the only one that persisted, "Jesus Christ?"

"Yes, Maka, wait till I tell you."

She absorbed every word as I explained the 'risen Christ'.

"That's wonderful," she exclaimed with tears welling in her eyes. "I want to know Him too."

"Maka, you have to give up reading tea leaves."

"Why?"

"The Lord is strongly opposed to that sort of thing. It'll get you into trouble."

"I didn't know that. Oh-h-h-h, I'll never do it again."

I knew she wouldn't even though people would come for miles to have their fortunes told by her.

A few months later we learned that she was in the hospital, recuperating from a massive heart attack. Our first opportunity to go to Windsor was for her grandson's wedding. I was seated in the second pew and before I could turn my head to see who was whispering so fervently in my ear, Maka had already related half the story of her death and meeting Jesus.

"S-h-h, wait till we get outside."

She was as jumpy and excited as a little kid, bending forward every few minutes to tell me more.

"Come, come you must hear what happened. Tom and Vera don't believe me. I SAW JESUS!"

"Start at the beginning, Maka."

"Okay. For three days before my heart attack, these shrouded figures kept coming into whichever room I was in and were calling my name, motioning me toward them. I didn't say anything, because, you know, you wonder if you're going a little funny. But now, listen to this, after three days of seeing these figures, I walked into my husband's bedroom and there was one of them sitting beside him, dressed in a black shroud. The bed was indented and sprang back when the figure rose. It rose and disappeared as soon as I came into the room. I knew my husband saw him also, because of the petrified expression on his face. He said, 'I'm going to die, they've come to get me!'

"I assured him that it wasn't him. They were after me. That same day I had my heart attack. I was laying on the floor and the three shrouded men stood and motioned with their hands for me to come with them, all the while calling my name, over and over. I remembered what you had said, to call on the name of Jesus. So I said, 'Jesus, Jesus, come to me.' HE CAME! I SAW HIM! He came and took my hand and asked if I wanted to go with Him. He was all shiny and glowing. I told Him I wanted to go with Him but that my husband was too old to take care of himself. The next thing I know, I woke up in the hospital.

"It happened, Donna, I did not dream this, He actually appeared to me."

"I believe you, Maka, I believe you. Praise God."

"Mother, did you hear that? Did you hear what she said?" I asked.

"Am I going to sit and listen to the ramblings of an old lady?"

"Old lady? You better take another look. That old lady, looks, dresses, carries herself and acts young enough to be your daughter. I suggest you start paying a little bit of attention to her, you might learn something."

I shared the concept of salvation with everyone I knew. I explained it was free for the asking. Submit your life to the Lord, sit back, and watch His perfect plan for your life unfold. Life, as it was meant to be lived.

Most seemed to accept what I was saying, but their response was, "That's just great, Donna. I'm glad it works for you. I don't need God or church right now. It's not for me." Yet these same people would complain day after day, "I have problems. I'm always tired. I don't feel good. My husband doesn't understand me; I think we're going to get a divorce. I think my wife's running around. My kid's dropped out of school."

Boy! I thought, do they need rejuvenation. Rejuvenation that comes from the Living God.

Others thought that running to Christianity was a 'cop out'. A COP OUT? Do you know how much guts it takes to be a Christian in this world of ours, today? Sheer guts! You think cowards stand up and tell today's society they love Jesus? Not very likely. I think blending into the crowd, having no backbone to stand up for anything, is the cop out. You believe you evolved from apes so you act like apes, anything goes. I believe a higher Omniscient Being created me in His own image and try daily to live up to that revelation.

Chris was the first to respond. Especially since she was so involved with her mother's psychic activities. I didn't hold back anything. I scared her half to death and insisted she renounce her participation in the supernatural. She came to church but was not impressed and decided to tune into the 700 Club, 100 Huntley Street and the PTL Club. She experienced the touch of God in the privacy of her own home. Hank was furious. Just as Darko, Hank had insisted God was a bunch of bunk, for little kids and mental midgets. He wouldn't allow us to ever discuss it in his presence. Even the expression 'Praise the Lord' would get a lifted brow and color would flush across his face.

Having found one friend, who gladly accepted that Jesus was very real and very accessible, I became bolder. My next door neighbor was complaining that her eighteen year old daughter slept till noon, hitchhiked all over the country till all hours of the morning, wouldn't go to school or get a job. She didn't know what to do with her. I attempted to share the Lord with her but she would have nothing to do with anything that wasn't Catholic.

"Forget about miracles, the power of prayer and the Holy Spirit." She went to church every Sunday and was an "I've got my ticket" Catholic, so instead, I called her daughter over that same day. She arrived after supper. I didn't know where to start, hardly knowing her, except to see her come and go occasionally. She was probably a lovely looking girl, but you couldn't tell. Her eyes were painted so black they looked like a raccoon's and her long thick hair might have been beautiful but it was teased so hard it stuck straight out, far from her head. She wore at least a dozen bracelets on each arm and a ring on every finger. You could see her coming a mile away.

I told her I had something to say, but that I didn't know how, so I wanted to play some video tapes I had recorded from the shows I had been watching. "Oh, I'm game, show me what you've got. I'm bored silly, anyway."

I first played a two hour tape on which Colonel Sanders of Kentucky Fried Chicken was giving his testimony about how he got saved. A tiny church was having a twenty-four hour prayer and fast vigil. They were praying for a millionaire. They had less than three days to come up with $36,000 or else they would have to close their doors. At the same time, Col. Sanders was driving by and the little white church on the hill beckoned him and drew him like a magnet. He circled back, and came through the doors. The pastor just motioned to him and said, "Come in, we've been expecting you. Come right up here. You are the answer to our prayers." That day he accepted the Lord as his Saviour, and of course, paid off the church debt.

He then proceeded to relate about the experience he had in the hospital when the doctors told him he had a cancerous polyp, which would have to be removed. He called for the minister, for a healing prayer, and knew beyond a shadow of a doubt that the polyp had passed through when he next went to the bathroom. He said nothing to the doctors and proceeded with the surgery only to wake up to find the doctor and six lawyers standing by his bed.

"We've made a mistake. There is no polyp."

"Don't worry guys, you won't be sued. I know I had one until last night, only Jesus beat you to the operation."

Lorrie didn't even blink. She just stared at my TV set.

"Do you want to see another one?" I asked, expecting her to say "no" and hightail it out as fast as she could.

She nodded her head up and down without saying one word. I put on the tape where Pat Boone related how his daughter's little white mouse had died. Pat Boone, being a giant in the faith, knew the power of prayer, knew Christians had dominion over the animals, so his little girl and he knelt and closed their eyes and committed that pet mouse to the Lord. When Pat opened his eyes, there was the little mouse, standing on his hind legs in the palm of his hand. Tears of joy and unbelief poured down their faces.

A veterinarian was on the same program saying how he stopped a charging bull, right in its tracks. The bull just slumped to the ground, merely feet from where he was standing frozen with fear. He said he prayed over each animal brought to his clinic. When asked by Jim Bakker if he told his clients that, he replied, "Are you kidding? Do you think they'd pay my phenomenal bill if they knew I only prayed over the animals?"

When the second tape was finished, I held my breath. She had placed her face in her hands and was quiet for about ten minutes. You could have heard a pin drop. When she lifted her head, her face was black with tears, "I understand now what the

'Jesus letters' from my brother are about. He's in prison in B.C. I just love him and he's been sending 'I love Jesus' and 'I've been saved' letters. We didn't know what he was talking about. Now I know. Now I understand. Oh Jesus! Hallelujah! I understand."

The Bible says, that their eyes would be opened and their ears unstopped by the word of God, and I was a witness to that very thing. She just went BINGO! I told her that to be born again and enter the kingdom of God you had to acknowledge that you were a sinner and that you believe that Jesus Christ died on the cross for those sins; you believe He rose from the dead and ask Him to come into your life as your Lord and Saviour. A simple prayer, yet it opens the gates of heaven and you become a child of God. We talked for hours.

"Can I come back tomorrow and talk some more? It's almost four in the morning?"

"Of course, any time. Whenever you want. Take this Bible and be sure to read it. It'll change your life."

And it did. The Holy Spirit changed her inside out. Within a week, she had stopped smoking. Her hair fell naturally in curls around her face. There was not a trace of makeup, and absolutely no jewellery but one ring and a chain around her neck. She WAS pretty. Really pretty. She found a steady job and was bubbling over with happiness . . . TALK ABOUT A NEW CREATURE!

Many evenings she came over and we would sit on my patio staring across the fields at the sunset, awestruck by God's handiwork.

After decades of groping in the dark of a busy world, Christians (I should say 'new' Christians) immediately stop to smell the flowers and start automatically to appreciate the beauty of nature. Her mother was not impressed.

"Look what's happened to her, Donna. No one would recognize her. No makeup. She just goes to work and reads her Bible. She's not the same person."

"Are you upset because she's finally acquired some good taste and doesn't look like she's going trick or treating or are you upset because she doesn't sleep till noon?"

"We're Catholic, Donna. It's wrong to leave the One True Holy Church."

"No one told Lorrie to quit smoking. Nobody told her that her makeup was hideous. The Holy Spirit showed her what needed attention in her life. She looks magnificent. She's deliriously happy. As for the One True Church, the only true church is the body of Christ; His believers. That's the only church the Bible professes."

"Holy spirit? Born again? I don't know what her father will do if she re-baptizes herself."

The next thing I knew, there was a 'For Sale' sign on their front lawn; and she was NOT listed with me.

June 1980

I was now making enough money that I realized I would need some expenses to offset the profit. Since my clients didn't appreciate climbing in and out of my two door, with a tiny back seat, I decided to shop for a larger car, with four doors. Darko agreed, but insisted it had to be a diesel. We didn't want another gas guzzler.

I must have priced at least fifteen cars, at as many dealers. Each dealer would have only one diesel on inventory and the price was standard, $13,500. There were not many options, either. I soon realized this was about $4,000 more than I could comfortably afford and almost gave up, when, driving by a dealer in Toronto, something kept telling me to stop, even though I was in a hurry for an appointment. I turned back and sought a salesman.

"Do you have a diesel, by any chance?"

"Sure do. What color did you have in mind?"

"You mean you have more than one?"

"As a matter of fact, we have thirteen."

"Do you have one in burgundy?"

"Right over here. Burgundy, inside and out. It's got air, power windows, opera windows, opera lights, AM-FM, digital clock and padded roof."

One look and I was sold.

"How much?"

"Let's see," he said while flipping some papers, "this one's $10,600."

"I'll take it." I responded on the spot. I knew a deal when I saw one. I also knew I'd have to sell at least one more house, to afford even that price. We were on a lease purchase with our Omnis and that was another problem. I explained my situation regarding the lease to the salesman. "I'll keep the car on ice for twenty-four hours. See if you can get out of your lease. I doubt you'll be able to."

I immediately drove to my dealer, praying all the way there. I knew the Lord wouldn't mind my upgrading my car for the convenience of my clients. Driving a tiny, two door, in real estate was very impractical.

"I'd like you to take this car back. How much will you give me for it?"

"You can't get out of a lease. Besides, we wouldn't give you any money, you'd have to buy the car out right, in full."

When I explained the car I had just seen, he couldn't believe it. "A car like that, without those options, costs the dealer more than $11,000. Just the 'diesel' option is $900 alone. It's impossible."

"If I prove to you that I'm telling you the truth, will you let me out of our lease?"

"You've got yourself a deal, lady, because I know it's impossible. You've made a mistake."

I dialed the Oldsmobile dealer and passed the phone to him. He was visibly upset.

I now had a problem I had not anticipated; putting out additional money on the car I was driving. I would definitely have to sell a house.

I did; that same evening. Unbelievable. "Thank you, Lord." I was amazed how He had worked out all the impossible details. Darko decided that he would keep my car and we would trade in his "024". Our dealer didn't care which lease he allowed us to terminate. When we went to take delivery the next day, I became suspicious of the salesman's math.

"Why would my monthly payments be that high?"

"There's tax included."

"Even with tax, you're still talking sixty dollars per month more than I've calculated. Times thirty-six months, that's more than two thousand dollars difference."

"To tell you the truth, I made a mistake yesterday. I quoted a price that was over one thousand dollars less than we paid for the car. I can't sell it at a loss. We just don't do that, especially with new cars."

"Well, we can't afford to buy it then." He didn't go for the threat, and actually let us walk away.

I was so disappointed. I figured the Lord was not behind this idea of mine and my clientele would have to suffer in my compact. Seven thirty, the next morning, I received a phone call from the manager of the dealership.

"Ma'am, I wouldn't want any bad publicity or want you to think that our salesmen quote one price to get you interested, then charge more once you've decided to buy. If my salesman said, $10,600, then that's what you'll pay. We'll take the loss and keep our good reputation. You may come and get your automobile."

This car fell right out of heaven as far as I was concerned. "We'll be right over."

Within hours, I was behind the wheel of my burgundy dream. . . thirty six miles per gallon, to boot!

The following Sunday, I sat in church wondering, "Why me, Lord? Why are you so good to me? Why?" I distinctly heard Him say, "I've blessed you more than abundantly."

Yes! But why? Tell me why. While I was sitting there, He showed me all the ways He'd blessed me, in this short period of time. I couldn't help but cry.

Pastor Fred was speaking about serving the Lord; finding something to do for Him, for His kingdom. What, I thought? I can't sing. I can't do anything. I don't want to take care of the babies in the nursery. I haven't been out of the diaper stage long enough to go back to changing more, but after pondering the idea, I decided to give the nursery a try. I presumed that it's the things that you do, that you don't like to do, that really count the most.

I signed up and the following Sunday morning I had a baby under each arm while trying desperately to hear the message on the the speakers which were simply not loud enough. At the conclusion of the service, a tall girl approached me to retrieve her baby from my arms.

"ARE YOU DONNA? DONNA MARTONFI?"

"Why yes, who are you?"

She was jumping up and down and hugging me. "Praise God! Hallelujah! My mother prayed for you. For year's my mother's been praying for you. Wait till I tell her. Praise God!"

"Who's your mother?" My mind raced, trying to figure out whom I had known that was born again.

"Don't you recognize me? I'm Sue, Verna's daughter. Verna's my mother."

That precious lady. I wouldn't go to Bible study with her so she spent years praying for me.

"It took you long enough! To think we'd meet here after all these years. Wait till she hears you're saved."

Donna before coming to Canada.

With her Dad in Toronto.

School days (Donna on right).

(April 1966) Donna and Darko with parents.

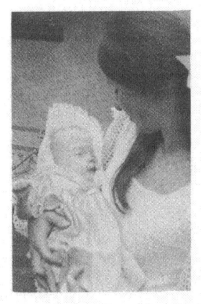

Diana just days before she died.

Their livelihood on wheels.

This is mommy's store.

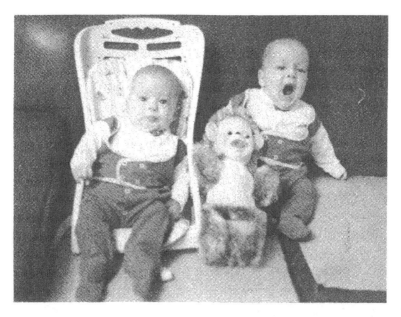

The astronaut (still yawning) beside brain surgeon.

More than a handful for Darko.

Michael, Danny and Stevie

"Baka Cica" Grandma Martonfi in costume with boys.

Learning to ride a bike was not the highlight of this day.

Donna after two years of hell on earth.

Sue, the real estate lady with the Bible in her purse.

Ben, he even tried to sell Canada.

Anna and Paul, there from the beginning.

Pastor Fred, not only a good friend but a good cook.

Donna's favorite relatives, Uncle Tom, Aunt Vera and Danny.

Joe, #1 Manager of the #1 office.

Fiona with her blessing.

Doug and Dorthy, clients that really got a deal.

Mike, Dan, Steve and Mom.

Donna and Darko — just beginning.

Chapter Nine

THINGS GO BETTER WITH GOD

I had found that the 'associate' position in a one man outfit was not working out and decided I'd go back to my former company where I had started originally.

Joe, the guy who had told me to go to church, had been promoted to manager of the new office, which was destined to be 'number one'. He handpicked his crew and wanted one great, big, happy, successful family.

"Congratulations, Joe, you deserve it."

"Thank you, Donna. You know I'd be more than pleased to have you join my office. You'll love the gang. They're really special."

"Joe, with your looks, you probably have a harem of thirty women over there," I teased.

"Oh, no, there's two guys," he shot back, oblivious to the fact that a parade of female agents were pounding at his door. "Ben's here too."

"If that's the case then I'm on my way." I liked the fast pace and was soon swept along with all the energetic positive agents who were scurrying to make his office famous. Joe motivated and energized us every Monday morning to sell, sell, sell and list, list, list. "List to last".

By Christmas, I was wondering why I was not reaping the rewards. I worked long and hard hours. I was a good agent and knew my stuff. Joe would laugh, "Donna, if you could talk as many people into buying homes, as you talk out of buying, you'd make 'agent of the year'. You're going to be the most loved agent, but also the most broke."

It was true. I was constantly telling someone that they were in no position to carry the heavy payments of the homes they were looking at, according to their incomes. "Buy a condo or a townhouse and work your way up."

The commission on a $35,000 to $40,000 condo is a lot, lot less than the commission on a $115,000 home. Twice that month I had arrived at the office to find a bouquet of flowers on my desk.

"Every time we see flowers on Donna's desk we know Donna didn't sell ANOTHER house," the agents quipped.

I considered that doing my job, though, warning young couples that were about to bite off more than they could chew.

"That's just fine, Donna. We know your honesty borders on stupidity, but you're making very little money.

I was satisfied. I didn't make fifty or sixty thousand a year but what I did make, for the effort that I put in, was more than sufficient.

We did list, list, list and were ready and stocked with "homes for sale" when the market really took off, a market that would go down in real estate history! Homes were going up thousands of dollars, daily. It seemed like half the city was for sale. I teamed up with a young rookie, who just got his license and didn't know the ropes. The first time I set eyes on him I knew Sue, now a close Christian friend, would really go for him. I was right, she did. They dated for over a year.

Our combination, although no one could figure out why, paid off big. We made a perfect team. In just one stretch of seven days, we listed and sold seven properties. Joe couldn't understand either, what it was that struck a match under me.

"Donna, I've never seen you go like this. Fantastic."

We worked night and day for forty-five days straight, without taking a break. Everyone knew this boom would not last long and each day meant an additional sale, or even two; if we were lucky. Each and every night we would be presenting offers or listing properties. It became phenomenal, only it was ten times more work, for only twice the amount of money.

On the same day that a home listed, we would arrive with an offer only to find that there were four or five in line ahead of us already. We would then have to wait our turn in the family room to present ours, sometimes waiting till three in the morning, and then find out that our "full price" offer was not acceptable; someone had bid higher than the asking price. Next day we would come back with $4,000 more than the asking price, and were still turned down.

We chased agents to see where they were hammering their 'For Sale' signs. No one bothered with MLS. By the time it hit MLS, it was already gone. We drove around with SIGNED offers in our pockets, just looking for the latest home to be put on the market. All we needed to do was find one and fill in the address on the Offer of Purchase and we would have ready made deals. Agents could not list the homes fast enough for the demand on the market. Many clients feared that if they didn't buy today, by next week they wouldn't be able to afford to buy a home.

I was determined that if this boom ever hit again, I would leave the country so I wouldn't be tempted into entering the chaotic race again. Agents were sleeping at the office, not even going home. Many were throwing up green bile from running on sheer nerves and black coffee. No one had time for a sit-down meal, and were grabbing quick bites between clients.

Our deals looked good on paper, but in the long run, it did not pay off. Nine times out of ten, you were selling some other agent's listing rather than your own. Out of 6% commission, half of it, (3%) goes to the company which has the 'listing' on the property. The remaining 3% is divided with your own company, leaving you only 1½%. When that is then divided with a partner, only 3/4 of 1% is left for you. That's NOT very much!

By August, the market was completely dead. Most agents were totally out of steam. Joe initiated a contest to motivate us. I was jolted by the Lord's stating: "Get up, be at your office by nine a.m. Now I'm going to show you how 'I' sell real estate."

"Okay Lord, I'm game."

I sat at my desk the next morning wondering if I had an overactive imagination. How could anyone sell real estate in this market?

My phone rang. "Is this Donna Martonfi?"

"Yes, may I help you?"

"Could you come over and list my house this afternoon?"

"Where did you get my name?" I asked, a little more than suspicious.

"From my friend, so-and-so. He recommended you highly."

"I can be over in about twenty minutes."

"Okay, fine. Thank you."

Wow! I'm actually going to get a listing. A listing was worth ten points. I'd at least get my name up on the score board. These contests always showed what you were made of; either you had it or you didn't.

When I arrived at the home, I was greeted by a very warm, hospitable couple. I took out my listing pad and asked for their mortgage papers. Nobody said, "Hold it!" or "We want to think about this." They simply proceeded to supply all the information I asked for. When I pushed the document toward them to sign, I was actually surprised when they both picked up a pen and endorsed it. This was too easy! Thank you, Lord! I see what you meant when you said, "watch Me sell real estate".

I happily called it a day and traipsed home to make an early supper, only to be called by the secretary later that evening saying an offer was registered and would I meet the agent at the house at 10:00 p.m. A sale? I had a sale? A sale would be another ten points. I'd be on top of the list!

When the agent handed me the offer, my heart sank. A $72,000 offer on a $97,000 home. "Are these people serious?" I fumed, thinking he dragged me out in the middle of the night for this absurd proposal.

"Don't go home, wait for me right here. I'll get a sign back."

"It had better be a lot better than this or else you're just wasting everyone's time."

"Don't worry, we'll have a deal."

Shortly after midnight he was back and I was pasting a 'SOLD' sticker on my sign.

The Lord's some real estate agent! He could list and sell a house in less than twenty-four hours. Boy, was I impressed!

"Be at your desk at nine a.m." He again urged.

'Why?' I thought. Before noon, I found out why.

"Is this Donna Martonfi?" the voice asked.

"Yes, may I help you?"

"Last night I saw a 'For Sale' sign across the street and this morning it said 'SOLD'. Now there isn't any sign. Did you sell that house in one day?"

"Yes, I did."

"Any agent that can sell a house that fast, in this market, I want to have working for me. Can you come over this afternoon?" I was astonished. Another ten points racked up. At this rate, no one in the office would be able to catch up to me.

By supper time I had thirty points and another "For Sale" sign up on a lawn. I phoned my first client and asked if he would put my sign back up, since it was the best form of advertising I could possibly have. The signs were located just kitty corner and could be seen all the way down the street.

"Lord, I don't know what to say, except, thank you. Thank you from the bottom of my heart."

"Be at your desk by nine a.m., tomorrow."

Why, wasn't I going to get a day off? I wouldn't have to go to work for a week, at this point. Unwillingly, I obeyed. At about the same time as the previous calls came in, a voice was asking, "Is this Donna Martonfi?"

I almost fell off my chair. I looked up to heaven, "I don't know if I can take much more of this, Lord".

"My street faces the two signs that you have on the other road. You seem to be the hottest agent in town, so I'd like you to come over and list my house."

I grabbed my briefcase and flew. My joy was soon squelched when I heard how much he wanted for his semi-- $121,000! For a semi? Ludicrous! Even in the boom, the most anyone had received for the largest of semis was only $105,000. It was a magnificent home, unbelievable in size and almost every square inch was covered in ceramics, but, even in a million years, it was not worth $121,000. Not only was he grossly overpriced, he was giving me only twenty-one days to sell it. He said he had placed a conditional offer on a new home and the builder would only give him twenty-one days to make it firm.

I knew that even the Lord couldn't sell that house, for that price, in twenty-one days yet. I agreed to take the listing only for the sake of the additional ten points. I insisted he give me a sixty day listing so that I could put it on MLS. Exclusive listings only received five points. At that high price, someone might suspect that I was getting a friend to list very high, so that I could get points, knowing he would never sell.

At forty points, I could take a month off.

"No. Be at your desk by nine a.m."

I just do not believe I'm going to pick up the phone again about 11:30 and be asked to come over and list another house. Come on now. . . I don't believe it.

Just in case, there I was.

>11:30...nothing!

>12:30... nothing!

>1:30..."Is this Donna Martonfi?"

The bottom fell out of my dream. This was all some big joke. Somebody put all these people up to calling me, to play a practical joke on me! None of this was real. It couldn't be. That first deal was not going to close, my signs would come down and I will have been played for a fool. It wasn't God at all. It was a big, bad, sick, joke. Who had I told that God was going to show me how 'He' sold real estate? No one. Not one soul. This joke was just inevitably timed properly.

"What can I do for you?" I asked sarcastically.

"I want to buy that house you listed last night."

"S-u--u-r-r-r-e you do. . . until you hear the price!"

"I don't care about the price, I want that house."

Since I had to return to get a signature from my client's wife, after her eleven p.m. shift, my sign didn't even go up until after midnight. "Oh really? Well tell me, just when did you see it? I checked my listing appointments this morning and no showings were registered. How is it that you want to buy a house you haven't seen?"

I wasn't stupid. There is a point to what I would believe. I couldn't believe he wasn't cracking up laughing right over the phone.

"I don't have to see it. I owned it two years ago, before I went to Italy and sold it to this guy for $115,000. Now I'm willing to buy it back for $115,000."

I cannot put into words the sensations that went through my body -- stronger than electrical charges, more potent than being hit by lightning. The presence of the Lord encompassed me.

"Why do you limit my capabilities? Why do you not believe?" He was asking. IT WAS GOD! HIS VOICE! HIS HANDIWORK!

I could hardly speak. . . "D-do y-y-ou want t-t-to come to my office and put in an offer?"

"Yes, I'll come over now. I want that house, Miss. I want you to get it for me and to get it for $115,000. I won't pay more than $115,000!"

It took days, but I haggled the vendor down to 115 and double ended the deal. (20 points)

Within ten days, I not only won the contest and had my picture in the paper as 'Agent of the Month', but I made almost more money than I had in any one year in real estate.

"Donna doesn't care what the market is doing, she creates her own boom."

"Joe, I finally made 'Agent of the Month'. I did it! My goal in real estate was to make it, at least once, Joe."

"Not just once, Donna, you have the capability, if you apply yourself, to be classed with the top agents in the country."

The Lord spoke again, "That's it! NO MORE. Now you will go home and take care of your family and MY business."

It made sense since Darko was recalled back to the company which had laid him off and was now working forty hours per week at BOTH places. That's eighty hours, week after week, not including traveling time. He couldn't decide which company to quit working for. He prayed daily for guidance from the Lord.

"Darko, it doesn't matter which place you work for, the Lord doesn't care. He'll bless you wherever you go." Since his seniority had been in effect throughout the layoff, he went with the first one. Within days of making the decision, he was offered the position of Maintenance Supervisor.

"Can you imagine. . . me. . . going to work in a shirt and tie?" That, I could imagine, but what I couldn't imagine was Darko with a dog, and I had decided to buy one. During the time I would spend at home, I could properly train it. I decided that the only way I could get one through the door would be to quit smoking in exchange. I found a cuddly, little, toy poodle. The kids were overjoyed. We had wanted a dog for a very long time and could never convince daddy to share his home with an animal. I was certain he would agree to the bargain.

I had bought a baby gate and put him in the back hall where he could see all the way down the hall. I was going to train him to be allowed only on the tiled areas of the house and stay off the carpeting. The upstairs would be completely off limits, meaning he would have access to 25% of the house. It was a pretty good compromise and Darko couldn't object with an arrangement like that. It's not as if I bought '86' dogs and was going to start a kennel.

I met him at the door with the good news, "Darko, I've quit smoking."

"Fantastic!"

"Come, look what I've bought with the money I'm going to save.

"Oh no. No. No. No. He has to go."

"Go? Why?"

"I'm not living in this house with a dog."

"He's not a D-O-G, dog; he's just a little thing. He can almost fit in the palm of your hand. He's not going to get much bigger. He doesn't shed, that's why I got him; it's not even fur! Have you ever seen anything so cute and adorable?"

"Keep him outside then."

"You can't keep a poodle outside. Say he can stay. You're not going to make me take him back? You just can't."

"I'm not coming downstairs till he's gone.

The kids and I were heartbroken. We decided Charlie was staying and daddy would eventually get used to him. I prepared Darko's favorite supper and called him downstairs.

"Is he gone?"

"No."

"Then I'm eating in a restaurant. I'm not sitting down to meals with a dog. He stinks."

"He doesn't stink. We'll give him a bath every day. I'll keep him in the family room when we eat. You sound like a typical Yugoslav!"

"That's just the point. I can name dozens of people that will never want to eat in our house ever again."

"Is that a promise?"

"He has to go."

I couldn't believe that little face didn't soften his heart. The next day, Darko again missed breakfast, lunch and went out for supper.

While he was gone the kids and I cut long sheets of wax paper and hung banners all over the kitchen. One had a picture of Charlie with big tears running down his face which read; "I don't like you much either, but I'm willing to live with you!" and "I'm cuter than most of your relatives!" Another showed the four of us with our hands in the air, praying, with the caption, "Whenever two or more agree as touching anything on earth, so it shall be done for them by my Father in heaven!"

I told the kids to pray without ceasing, asking the Lord to change his heart and allow Charlie to stay. He didn't come into the kitchen but went straight out the door.

The third morning he came home, saw the banners, broke out in a grin and said, "I can say 'no' to you. I can say 'no' to the kids, but when God starts asking me to let you have the dog, I guess I can't argue. Just don't call him FiFi. I'm not living under the same roof with a Fifi-sa."

He turned out to be the best dog anyone could hope to have. He wasn't yappy, easily trained, obeyed his boundaries in the house and even knew where the boundary to our acre was outside. We never had to tie him up, he'd stay on the property.

Now the kids and I didn't spoil that dog, but every time Darko had a bite to eat, Charlie would get a huge morsel. I didn't think I'd live to see the day Darko would be romping around our yard, chasing and playing with a tiny poodle. WHY don't people out there believe in miracles?

Chapter Ten

SO UNBELIEVABLE -- IT´S BELIEVABLE

Realizing I was needed at home temporarily, I gladly took the time off. I pondered over what the Lord had said concerning "His business". Coincidentally, the topic that Sunday was, 'What We Can Do for God's Kingdom'. One thought, 'Go to the little Catholic church', kept surfacing constantly.

"I can't go to the Catholic church. For what? What would I do?"

Again and again, "Go to the little Catholic church. The priest asked you to come back and help them."

"Help them what?" I argued. "I don't know anything. I can't quote scripture. I don't even know scripture. I'm not equipped to teach anyone anything."

All night I argued back and forth in my head, not once thinking I was arguing with God. It hadn't even crossed my mind that He was asking me to do something. I couldn't get to sleep for hours. In the morning, Darko burst through the bedroom door, "Donna! Donna, wake up! God spoke to me! Are you awake? Listen!"

"I'm awake, I'm awake!"

"A few of us gathered to pray at work and God spoke to me. It's like there was a sheet of paper in front of my face. I could read the instructions."

"What did He say?" I didn't know why I was so surprised that the Lord would speak to Darko. It certainly was a little out of the norm.

"You have a mission. Listen!"

"Don't tell me, I KNOW. He wants me to go to the Catholic church; right?"

"How did you know?" he questioned, absolutely amazed.

"I guess He's been talking to me too, only I've been arguing with Him."

We immediately went downstairs to phone the priest who had asked me to come back. I was given the names of the people to contact who had organized 'Renew' meetings throughout the community. They were excited by my story and asked me to come out that same evening and join in their program.

All day, I wondered what I was to say or do once I got there. A scripture helped! "But the comforter, which is the Holy Ghost, whom the Father will send in my name, He shall teach you all things, and bring all things to your remembrance, whatsoever I have said unto you." (John 14:26).

Once there, it became immediately apparent how far I had actually come. These people were genuine and sincere, but they completely missed the mark. One of the questions on their program, after the story of Jesus and the prostitute was; 'What do you suppose He was writing in the sand with His finger?'

The Scribes and the Pharisees had brought Jesus a prostitute demanding that she be stoned. Jesus ignored them and stooped and wrote in the sand with His finger. They persisted. He rose and said, "He that is without sin among you, let him first cast a stone at her". And they which heard it, being convicted by their own conscience, left one by one, beginning at the eldest, even unto the last. Jesus and the woman were left alone and He said unto her, "Woman, where are those thine accusers? Hath no man condemned thee?" She said, "No man, Lord." and Jesus said unto her, "Neither do I condemn thee; go, and sin no more".

"Who cares what He was writing? If He wanted you to know He'd have told you." I also couldn't resist the quip, "Maybe it was the names of women that the Pharisees had known; that's why they left one by one."

The Lord then anointed my mouth and I spent almost the whole hour teaching on Christ and the message in the above scripture; truths that most had never heard. I was amazed myself at the knowledge that was pouring from my lips.

I was asked to come to the Friday afternoon prayer meetings, which the leaders of the various groups held. I gladly accepted. I had not suspected, even dreamed, that these women prayed in tongues, knew about the movement and baptism of the Holy Spirit and believed in faith healing.

"Why don't you tell the people in the congregation these things? They are as clueless as I was. There is a whole spiritual world out there that Catholics don't even know exists. Why doesn't the priest shout this from the pulpit? Why is it a secret?"

"It's not for everyone, only for the ones that are chosen," came the incredible reply.

"And who chooses? Who decides who is to be enlightened, and who is to be left in the dark? These people are coming to the meetings obviously because they are hungry for more of God."

"If the priest spoke of these things on Sunday, people would go running for the doors. The church would be vacated."

"Just the opposite, it would be bursting at the seams. I didn't go to church because I would walk out just as dead and void as when I entered, until someone showed me the 'Living God' ", I affirmed, somehow, still believing that they were on the right track.

"It's not up to us or the priest. We go according to the Vatican and the Holy Father."

Before I left, I was asked to give a five minute speech at one of the Masses, encouraging more people to join the weekly meetings. Since Darko and I had booked a trip to Barbados, I decided it would be an opportune time to write and practice my speech on the flight down. The fact that I would stand up, in front of hundreds of strangers, and talk, was more of a miracle than being able to actually afford a winter trip to the islands.

I was informed that I would be speaking the very morning after my return. Both of our mothers volunteered to be there.

Our plane arrived much later than anticipated, well past midnight. I was extremely nervous. Would I actually be able to speak in front of an audience? What if I froze? Just the opposite happened. I talked so fast that I was finished the following speech in less than two minutes.

"Good Morning;

You know the trouble with being asked to speak? If I had been asked this morning, I could have probably barely managed three minutes, — but, I can come up with three minutes worth of ideas per day, and I was asked over three weeks ago, so-o-o I hope you people have 'till 4:30!"

(Nobody laughed. It was 11:00 in the morning and I threatened to speak till 4:30 and NOBODY laughed. I talked faster.) "I thought I was a good little Christian. As far back as eight years ago, I was asked by various people and friends to go to prayer meetings or bible study. ON TUESDAYS? God was lucky when I got there on Sundays! My clients would think I'm a religious nut. They might even stop buying houses from me. Would you believe, now I go to the morning and the evening service on Sundays, PLUS two meetings per week, and many of my clients are right there with me.

"I used to refer to God as the 'Man Upstairs', busy sitting on a cloud while I'm busy FORCING life down here. Also, that He only answered when He felt like it, sometimes at the very last minute, and that He sometimes ignored me completely. Then I met Christ and His Word. Now, I can't imagine how a person could function and exist without Christ. He's changed my life. HE'S ALIVE! HE'S REAL! HE HAS A HOLD OF MY HAND – A good, real, strong hold!

"In the past two years, our family has LEARNED TO LEAN ON JESUS. Learned the importance of Christian fellowship sharing God and most importantly — the power of prayer. HE ALWAYS listens. There is ALWAYS an answer. You are never ignored when you call on Christ. He rose from the dead and is as close as the mention of His name.

"Since then, my kids think they've already died and gone to heaven. Our Bible is alive and talks and breathes. There is a communication — a telephone line to heaven. I'm convinced people hunger and thirst for God, but don't realize it themselves, until someone breaks the ice. Until someone shows them what it's all really about.

"Christian fellowship is invaluable. Putting Christ in your home, your business, school and family relationships is rewarding beyond comprehension — it truly brings a peace that surpasseth all understanding. It fills a gap that you were born with but sometimes don't realize is there, until that gap is filled and you experience TRUE JOY. TRUE LIFE, as it was meant to be lived, in union with God.

"You have to take the first step towards God. He does the rest, jumps off that cloud and into your everyday worries, problems, and life.

"My husband and I intend to write a book, but the past two years could already fill a library. We've been blessed right out of our socks. I really could go on for hours — I won't — I'm hungry too!

"God's brought so much meaning into our lives and the lives of people around us. Our happiness has been contagious. We've put our burdens and problems at His feet and He's been quick to take them from us. People have said I'm the lady who gets such a kick out of her religion — but now I can't get a word in edgewise with them. Praise God.

"I know to some of you this is all very frightening because you're too busy for God. 'Just leave Him in Heaven for now, maybe next year. . . When I have more time. . . I don't even get to see much of my friends, let alone go to meetings'. But I know He's standing, calling your name, probably for years, as in my case, and HE MAKES TIME — rewarding, heavenly time. You'd be surprised how much time you do have. Please, at least try it.

"TAKE THAT STEP."

To my astonishment, my mother-in-law said, "Congratulations, Dana, that was excellent. Very well said."

"I spoke too fast. Could anyone understand me?'

"It was perfect," she insisted, "Just perfect."

This must have been the first nice thing my mother-in-law ever said to me.

I couldn't wait for the following Tuesday, to be able to enlighten the dozen or so that came to these meetings, hungry for more of God. That Tuesday turned out to be a nightmare. Instead of seeking the face of God, praying or sticking to the program prepared, I couldn't keep them from discussing menus, talking about washing their cars and complaining about the weather; except for one girl.

She returned willingly, time and again, to the topic at hand. I made a mental note to zero in on her next week.

I kept my Friday appointments with the leaders. The days in between, I spent absorbed in the Word. The Lord was revealing so much, so quickly, and He always prepared me for the next topic of discussion. I would practically know, before I arrived, what questions would arise from the discussion. They would be questions to which the Lord had prepared my answers. It never failed.

The following week, I did zero in on Fiona. Her eyes would just light up at any truth that I would share. The leader, I was certain, by this point, was instructed to keep me in line.

"What's charismatic?" Fiona asked.

"It's a type of chiropractor," laughed the leader.

"Baptism of the Holy Spirit?" Fiona questioned.

Again, a smart aleck reply from the leader, while at the same time she motioned to me with her hand not to dare reveal any more. I had said enough, as far as she was concerned.

The Lord had revealed plenty through me that night, regardless. I was utterly amazed that I knew precisely where truths were in the Bible and could turn to them easily. I revealed a lot more than the leader had anticipated. I again felt the anointing of the Holy Spirit, all around me. I could feel Him moving. It was breathtaking, especially for me; I was shy of strangers and here I was, center stage, preaching.

Now I must explain that I am not a SHY person, nor am I ever short on words. My nickname is 'motormouth'. It just takes me a long time to open up, in front of strangers, but when I do, look out, there is just no stopping me.

"Fiona," I approached her after the meeting, "would you like to go for a coffee, somewhere?"

She gladly agreed, saying her husband was taking care of her son and she was not in any hurry.

Once at the donut shop, I proceeded to tell her about the Lord, from A to Z, my experiences, everything. We were there about three hours, making it now past one in the morning!

She was awestruck. "You're story is so unbelievable, it's believable." Her ears strained for more.

"I go to a church where people believe so strongly and deeply that they aren't ashamed to join hands in public, and pray out loud."

"Oh, you wouldn't here? Not now," looking sheepishly around. "Oh don't do that here. Okay?"

I told her about the charismatic meetings that I heard the Catholics were holding somewhere in Mississauga.

"I'd really like to go, really I would. I'm not just saying that. I would really like to go to one. Could you find one for me?"

I would have to find one. It would be perfect. I couldn't very well go to a Catholic meeting and drag people off to my church. That would be too obvious, but I could lead them to their own charismatic movement.

I found one that was being held on Monday evenings and arranged to take Fiona the following Monday. She cried, she waved her arms in the air and cried some more. "Thank you, thank you, Jesus" she sobbed. Hugging me she kept repeating, "Thank you, Jesus."

"Fiona, now do you want to come and see the REAL thing?" I asked.

"The real thing?"

"Yes. They've got the right idea and they're on the right track, but, it's so mechanical, not the Spirit of God moving at all, as He wants to."

Tuesday night, Fiona and I were both leading the meeting. We made a great team. She was telling of how much more there was of the Lord than people realized and how she was touched by Him.

Well, on Sunday, at my church, she was more than touched. She lit up. Finally, someone I had brought, LIT UP. To be more descriptive, she was turned inside out.

"Where has this been all my life? Why didn't I know God before?"

"That's funny, Fiona, that's the same question I asked."

Man from birth, has four crucial requirements for his well-being and development; 1) love/companionship, 2) food, and 3) shelter. They are adequate to exist meagerly. To live in utmost joy and satisfaction, he also needs to have his spiritual requirements met. Inside every human being is a void in the shape of Christ, that only Christ can fill. From the day he is born, that longing is present, though many never understand what it is. That yearning needs to be completely satisfied. He cannot experience the abundance and full satisfaction life has to offer unless that void is filled. Why else would millionaires, having fame, fortune, mates and families, everything this world has to offer, commit suicide, become alcoholics or resort to drugs? Obviously, they long for more than the emptiness they found at the top of the heap. They know the disappointment of finding that material goods don't satisfy nor give them inner peace.

I decided that two heads were better than one and invited Fiona to join the Friday prayer meeting with the leaders. Actually, I think at times I felt intimidated and outnumbered, and an extra believer on my side would soften the blows. I instructed her on how I was treading carefully, not disputing any of their false doctrines, but contributing 'truth' by my abstention from anything that was contrary to scripture.

At her introductory meeting, Fiona soon realized how sensitive and delicate the situation could become. One of the leaders asked point blank, why I refrained from praying the 'Hail Mary' in unison with them. I explained that the Lord commanded, in many, many places in scripture, to pray to Him alone and to no one else. I shed light on the fact that Catholics had omitted the 'second' commandment, in all of their literature and teaching, and replaced it by making the tenth commandment numbers nine AND ten.

The second reads: "Thou shalt have no other god than me. Thou shalt not make unto thee any graven image, or any likeness of any thing that is in heaven above, or that is in the earth beneath, or that is in the water under the earth; thou shalt not bow down thyself to them nor serve them; for I the Lord thy God am a jealous God, visiting the iniquity of the fathers upon the children unto the third and fourth generation of them that hate me" (Exodus 20: 3-5).

"That's a pretty heavy commandment, the Lord saying if you worship any other than Him alone, that you hate Him."

They told me that I had been misled and urged me to pray fervently about it even though their own Bibles contained that commandment. I was handed two books to read, about the appearances of the Virgin Mary, all over the world.

My first thought after reading this literature was to phone Pastor Fred and get all the answers for these "elect" of the church, but the Lord stopped me short; "Find out for yourself, on your own, so that no one can deter you from your belief. You obey My word, not a religion's belief, not a pastor's. You will go directly to MY source".

I did much searching through the scriptures. Hours and hours. By the end of the week I had typed a synopsis. I was really worried about my next meeting with these five ladies. As I read my Bible and prayed about my concern, and my actual fear of these women, the word 'Elijah' became alive on the pages. It wasn't familiar to me and I wondered if I had ever read it. Again and again, Elijah would leap off the pages at me.

"All right. All right, Lord, I'll look up the story of Elijah."

The story happened to be about Elijah coming against the 850 false prophets of the god Baal, and how he defeated them through the intervention of God Almighty.

Oh, how God answers prayer. He led me directly to the one passage that would speak directly to me and the circumstance I found myself in. Here I was afraid of five little Catholic women, when I had all the power of the Lord within me.

I zealously headed to the meeting and handed everyone a copy of my synopsis.

"I have given you the courtesy of reading your pamphlets; I would appreciate the same courtesy returned, and ask that you peruse the following, taken from the Bible:

"THE TWO PAMPHLETS, REPORTING THE APPEARANCES OF THE VIRGIN MARY ARE COMPLETELY CONTRARY TO HER CHARACTER:

In Luke 1:46-55 her character is best defined and expressed when she prayed the 'Magnificat'

—my soul doth magnify the Lord

—God my Saviour (She needed a saviour as does all mankind)

—and holy is HIS name (His name, not her name)

—mercy from generation to generation (meaning forever, even 1980. Jesus does not stop being merciful so that we have to appeal to His mother)

—He hath exalted them of low esteem (He, not 'I')

—He hath filled the hungry with good things (Again 'He')

The Virgin Mary in your pamphlets states;

—'I' am the virgin of the poor ???

—Reserve this spring for 'me', to relieve the sick (Her spring will relieve the sick? Jesus said, "He who does a miracle in 'MY' name." There is healing in the name of Jesus; not Mary.

—I would like a shrine — for people to worship and pray to 'ME'! (again, read the second commandment)

—I come to relieve suffering ???

—I am the mother of God ??? He would then also have aunts and uncles. She was the mother of Jesus only.

Not only is the above completely contrary to the nature of the mother of Jesus, but please read the following passages:

Matthew 4:10— and only Him shalt thou worship

Matthew 12:50 — when the disciples advised Jesus his mother wanted to see him outside, He replied, 'For whosoever shall do the will of my Father which is in heaven, the same is my brother, and sister, and mother.'

(Is He saying we are all God's Mother and should be worshipped and prayed to?)

Matthew 18: 19 and 20 'Where two or more are gathered in MY NAME, there am I in the midst of them.' (In HIS name, not the saints'; NO OTHER NAME BUT HIS)

Luke 11:27— A woman in a crowd said to Jesus, 'blessed is the womb that bore thee, and the paps which thou hast sucked.' NOTICE VERSE 28! Jesus replied, 'Yea, RATHER, blessed are they that hear the word of God, and keep it!'

Luke 21:8 — 'Take heed that ye be not deceived, for many shall come IN MY NAME'

Matthew 24:24 — FOR THERE SHALL ARISE FALSE

CHRISTS, AND FALSE PROPHETS, AND SHALL SHOW

GREAT SIGNS AND WONDERS: IN SO MUCH THAT, IF IT

WERE POSSIBLE, THEY SHALL DECEIVE THE VERY ELECT

(of God), verse 25— BEHOLD I HAVE TOLD YOU BEFORE

(Is that or is that nor a warning!?).''

I added that I did not believe that Jesus' mother was appearing in various places all over the world. As scripture points out; even Satan can disguise himself as an angel of light and his ministers as ministers of righteousness; and suggested they read 2 Corinthians, chapter 11, on false leaders and teachers. Also especially significant is the verse where Jesus is dying on the cross, Mary is before Him, and He addresses her as 'WOMAN' (John 19:26). Not Holy Mary; not Mother of God! Not Immaculate Heart! Simply, and only, woman; showing future generations that she was only a mortal, NOT DEITY. A saint, just as every believer is, in the body of Christ. Not superior and not to be prayed to.

When I had finished, the quiet in the room was absolutely deafening. I silently prayed that the Spirit of God would convict their hearts of this very important truth. The Spirit WAS at work. That was obvious. When we held hands and prayed, I could feel energy, as electricity, flowing and exiting out of the tips of my fingers.

The person holding my hand noticed it too. She jerked and let go and pulled her hand away as if she got a shock.

Lorrie asked if she could join Fiona and myself any time we went to the Charismatic Meetings. One particular night, Lorrie brought a girl named Robin with her, who was from this very same parish. I immediately grew suspicious of her. She asked such point blank questions, that I was certain she was a 'plant'. I dodged her questions meticulously, only to have Fiona notice my answers were too general and evasive, so she attempted to elaborate. A sharp jab to the ribs was enough to warn her that there was something not right. I waited to get her alone, in private.

"Fiona, I don't trust her. Her questions are so precise and rehearsed, that I suspect she was coached and has been sent to find out what we're up to and where I'm coming from. Say nothing about doctrinal issues and don't mention that you've been to my church."

Fiona agreed that her questions were more than just mere curiosity, shooting out one after the other.

"Didn't you have to sign some sort of card when you became a member of the Pentecostal church?" she'd ask. "Are you against all the saints then? Are you against the Pope? Why do your pastors marry? Why don't you have communion each week? Are you forbidden to make the sign of the cross?" On and on and on.

Finally, I decided to take my chances and give her the whole story.

"Robin, the card we sign is something to the effect of 'I believe that Jesus Christ is the Son of God and that He was crucified and rose from the dead, I have asked Him into my life and I am also willing to be baptized.' That's all, nothing secretive. As for the saints, Robin, each and every believer and follower of Jesus Christ becomes a saint, we are joined to the body of Christ. To pray to Saint Anthony or Saint Peter is as wrong as to pray to each other or worship each other. These attitudes and actions are to be bestowed only to God and our Lord Jesus Christ."

She made no comment, so I continued, "As for communion, we are encouraged by our Lord, to do this in remembrance of Him, His broken body and blood that He shed for us. It is not to become a daily, meaningless ritual but something to be celebrated with anticipation and expectation. Also Robin, I want you to understand that as Christians, or Pentecostals, or 'Born Again' believers, we are not 'forbidden' to do anything. Jesus gave two commandments; that we love God with all our hearts, and that we love one another as He loved us. Through our belief in Jesus Christ, we are adopted into the family of God and into everlasting life. Any sin that is committed will be forgiven by God. Naturally, you could say that dabbling with the occult or astrology is forbidden, but only because once you are on the road to the supernatural, you are moving away from the Lord and not many find their way back. Still we don't use the word forbidden as the Catholics do."

I was exhausted and relieved when she left.

As it turned out, some weeks later, Robin became born again, and we all laugh to this day that we had suspected her of being a spy.

Fiona worried out loud about what lay ahead, "Donna, what are we going to do now?"

"Nothing. We'll just go tomorrow night and preach the word of God and make known as many truths as we can."
Two of the top leaders were at that meeting. Even though I knew this to be unusual, I carried on for about an hour and a half. The response was dynamic with many asking profound questions and showing that they were grasping the 'truth' of scripture and the plan of salvation. Then the bomb fell. The main leader, or 'Big Wig', threw her Bible through the air and nastily exclaimed, "Why, this is nothing but a glorified history book."

One statement, coming from whom it did, nullified the entire message of that evening.

"What is there to believe then? What is there to base your faith on, if not on the 'Infallible Word of God', which is what Christians call that book?"

I received no reply.

I was dumbfounded. If a 'pillar' in the Catholic church could throw the Bible around and call it a history book, how could I hope to inspire the people to the truths which it contained.

Now I was ready for battle. In the meetings that followed, I started throwing some heavies around, right where I knew it counted.

"Did you know that Peter was married?" I pointed out. "He had a wife AND a mother-in-law. That's why we believe that priests can marry. God ordained the family. He approves and blesses the family unit. One of the ways scriptures show us how to judge our ministers is by how well they care for their own families."

"He couldn't have been married!" the response came from most everyone there.

"He was. Look in your Bible," I replied, knowing very well the questions that would now arise in their minds.

"But he was the first Pope!"

"No, he wasn't. There were no popes for 590 years. Gregory I, called Gregory the Great, was the first. He turned the church on a new course and is the founder of the papal monarchy. There were no churches even until Constantine, in the year 310. The Christians met in their homes because they were not allowed to build churches and they preached the 'Good News' outside of the Jewish synagogues. When Constantine allowed them to have their own churches, many pagans entered, bringing with them many pagan customs and statues which were then incorporated into the church. It became corrupted and paganized."

The response came as I had hoped, "But Jesus said that upon Peter He would build His church."

"No He didn't. You are referring to the statement, 'Upon this rock I will build my church'. After that statement, Jesus also said to Peter, now the alleged pope, 'Get thee behind me Satan'. Would this be any way to talk to the new pope? Also, shortly after, Peter fearfully denied Christ upon His arrest. Would the infallible pope have been a coward? What sort of example would that be setting? What Jesus said was that upon this rock (this truth — that He was the Christ, the son of the Living God), He would build His church. In Hebrew, Peter's name had been changed, by the Lord, to "stone" or "pebble", but Jesus used the Hebrew word 'ROCK' when referring to what He would build His church upon, against which the gates of hell would not prevail. The church would not remain standing long if He had built it upon Peter. Besides, we are His church, the body of Christ. He was not referring to buildings.

"Peter never claimed to have any authority or claimed to be pope. He refers to himself as an apostle of Jesus Christ and refused to accept homage from Cornelius, saying he was merely a man. The other apostles seemed unaware of any appointment that made Peter the head of the church. He was never sent to Rome to preach nor does scripture ever mention Peter being in Rome, while it does record Paul's journey to that city in great detail. Yet Catholics claim that Peter founded the church in Rome and presided over it for twenty-five years. Also, he was the apostle to the Jews, not to the Gentiles. Paul was the apostle to the Gentiles, by divine appointment. When he was dying he made no mention of choosing his successor or how to appoint another successor which would have been very relevant, had he been the first pope."

I could see the wheels turning. Many started to think for themselves, to reason for themselves. I knew that they would go home and start searching their Bibles, now that it was pointed out to them, just what was in it. The pope was not infallible, the Word of God was infallible.

Interestingly enough, the following week the passage on the program ended at Colossians 2:17. I pointed out verses 18 and 19 (TLB): "Don't let anyone declare you lost when you refuse to worship angels, as they say you must. They have seen a vision, they say, and know you should. These proud men (though they claim to be so humble) have a very clever imagination. But they are not connected to Christ, the Head to which all of us who are His body are joined; for we are joined together by His strong sinews and we grow only as we get our nourishment and strength from God."

Again there was a very long silence. (A nun had joined this particular meeting).

The questions in the program had also completely missed the teaching of the scripture just before the one above. Since the leader was not throwing any light on the subject, I again started:

"God Almighty not only forgives your sins, but blots them out and forgets them altogether, when you ask for forgiveness. When you come to Him through the cross of Christ, you are perfect and spotless before Him."

"We can never be perfect", argued the nun.

"We are perfect in God's eyes when we come through the blood of Christ. That was the purpose of His death, to reunite us with God. To pay the ultimate penalty for the sins of man; something we could never do. You have been taught that you have to go to purgatory to pay for your sins. There is no such place anywhere in the Bible. It's a fabricated place thought up by Plato, centuries before Christ, which was adopted by the people of India, Persia and Egypt."

"I always thought of Christ as being behind us, keeping us from hell", she persisted.

"Not at all, He's the mediator BETWEEN man and God, joining and reuniting us to God. See what verse eight says:

'Don't let others spoil your faith and joy with their wrong and shallow answers built on men's thoughts and ideas, instead of on what Christ has said'"

"I don't agree with you, Donna, but something inside of me tells me it's somehow right and that I should go home and pray about it," she said sweetly.

Thank God! I'm getting through. The Holy Spirit is talking to their hearts, dismantling years of man-made doctrine. I continued, "Further in Chapter Two, starting at verse 20; 'Since you died, as it were, with Christ and this has set you free from following the world's ideas of how to be saved — by doing good and obeying various rules — why do you keep right on following them anyway, still bound by such rules as not eating, tasting, or even touching certain foods? Such rules are mere human teachings, for food was made to be eaten and used up. These rules may seem good, for rules of this kind require strong devotion and are humiliating and hard on the body, but they have no effect when it comes to conquering a person's evil thoughts and desires. They only make him proud. Since you became alive again, so to speak, when Christ arose from the dead, now set your sights on the rich treasures and joys of heaven, where He sits beside God in the place of honor and power. Let heaven fill your thoughts; don't spend your time worrying about things down here. You should have as little desire for this world as a dead person does. Your real life is in heaven with Christ and God. And when Christ, who is our real life comes back again, you will shine with Him and share in all His glories!"

I did not know until the following Friday, just how much the Holy Spirit had been speaking to their hearts. Upon arriving, the 'second in command', not stopping to start the meeting with prayer, blasted me before I could sit down.

"You are dangerous, Donna! This rubbish actually got to me; I had stopped saying my rosary. . . (I had defended myself the Friday before when I said, not only would I not pray to anyone other than the Lord, but ten 'Hail Mary's' to every one 'Our Father', I thought more than disrespectful) . . . I was vacuum cleaning just yesterday when I fell on my knees and asked the Holy Mother for forgiveness."

PRAISE GOD!, I thought. If I could get her to stop saying her rosary, just think of the impact on the others!

The 'first in command' now turned to Fiona and asked, "Why don't you make the sign of the cross, Fiona?"

Fiona, still sitting on the fence, replied, "Because Donna doesn't."

No! No! that was not the thing to say.

"Precisely," continued Numero Uno, "Donna doesn't even wear a crucifix. She has the world hanging around her neck. I wear a crucifix to show the world I'm a Catholic."

"I hope I'll never have to wear an outward sign to show the world I belong to Christ," I replied, but my words went right over their heads. "Besides, don't you think it's about time you let Him off that crucifix. He's not hanging there anymore."

"Only when the Pope takes him down. Since he's infallible, what he says goes."

"One Pope, John XI, was the illegitimate son of Pope Sergius III. Pole Alexander VI had six illegitimate children. Another twenty-nine popes are listed as anti-popes and are said to have obtained the office by fraud. Are you going to wait a hundred years and learn that this pope has been denounced and that you have been living your life offending God? That's why the Lord gave us His instruction manual, so that man could not tamper with His will and instigate his own rules and regulations."

The subject was dropped.

I only then noticed that there was an addition to the prayer meeting. I had hoped that she had digested what had transpired. Eventually, somebody had to open their eyes and their minds to adhering to the word of God.

"I would like to be baptized by the Spirit. I accepted the Lord last week", she professed.

After everyone had laid hands on her and were praying, she was instructed to go home and practice a word, 'Yanehoya' or something to that effect, over and over, with the promise that she would be speaking in tongues by the end of the week.

I was mortified. This was as bad as the night Fiona and I were at the charismatic meeting and they had announced that there was going to be a seminar on 'Learn How To Heal'. The two of us immediately started making arrangements to sign up when I received a hard kick, to my rear, through the opening of the stacking chair I was sitting on. We were in the last row and I was stunned to see absolutely no one behind or near me.

"YOU DO NOT LEARN TO HEAL, IT IS A GIFT FROM ME!"

"Fiona, the Lord just kicked me! We can't go."

"What?" she looked as surprised as if He'd just kicked her too.

"First you learn how to heal, then you learn how to pray in tongues. Pretty soon they won't need God at all!"

I decided that I should discuss the tongues issue with Pastor Fred.

"Donna, that is so close to the Hindu religion, chanting a mantra, dulling their minds with a monotone rhythm. I wouldn't be surprised if she DID come back talking in sentences next week, only, it's NOT of God. Anything genuine has a counterfeit. Let's pray for them."

The weekly Tuesday meetings had ended for the season but Fiona and I attended the leader's prayer sessions, regardless, not realizing this was to be our last time.

"Unless you make the sign of the cross right here and right now and join in our prayer to the Holy Mother, you are not welcome here anymore and you certainly would be barred from attending further 'renew' meetings", we were bluntly informed.

"I have never asked you not to make the sign of the cross or stopped you from praying any way you wished. It is your prerogative, you are not convicted that it is wrong, but I will not conform to anything that contradicts the Bible."

"CAN IT! JUST CAN IT DONNA!"

The gal who had been baptized in the spirit the week before was screaming, "I DON'T WANT TO HEAR ANY MORE ABOUT THE STUPID BIBLE!"

"Why do the five of you each have one open on the table then?"

"I SAID CAN IT!" she was yelling and screaming so loud you could hear her three doors away. No one even tried to restrain her. Her eyes were wild. Fiona looked frightened. I lowered my eyes and silently prayed, "Heavenly Father, forgive them their trespasses, for they know not what they do."

Outside. . . "PRAISE THE LORD, Fiona! Satan doesn't attack anything that he doesn't fear. Praise God, we must be stepping on the devil's toes."

Still, it bothered me that I wasn't coming back. Now what? God told me to go into the church almost a year ago and now they've thrown me out. Now what?

I decided to drive to Jenny's. She was the warmest, sweetest and most gentle woman God ever created. Her eyes were penetrating and held wisdom nothing short of one that might be a thousand years old. Maturity radiated from her face which shone in a true Christ-likeness.

Jenny and Gord had purchased a house from me, not too far from where we lived. When I brought the vendors Jenny and Gord's offer, there were two other offers on the same property, one being higher than their's. The vendors said that they could not think of anyone they would rather have buy their home, than my clients and wanted to sell to them; as they were such gracious and lovely people. After moving in, they sent me a thank you card which read: 'It's not what you did, but how you did it.' Imagine, a real estate agent getting a thank you note!

They became very precious friends and I wanted to now seek her advice.

"It seems like the Lord's closed the door, Donna. Your assignment is completed. Another will water what you have sown and yet another will reap. You've done all you can."

Chapter Eleven

BE PATIENT -- GOD´S NOT FINISHED WITH ME YET

Joe's office was having another contest. This time the prize was a trip to the Bahamas.

"Are you ready to work, Donna?" Joe asked.

"I don't know," I teased, "I've still got my tan from Barbados. I don't know if I can handle two trips in one year."

The mortgage we held was maturing in the spring. There was really nothing to motivate me to work night and day other than the fact I wanted to look good in an office now filled with successful agents. I didn't want to look like a loser, a label many in the profession applied to Christians.

"They become a Christian and lose that 'killer instinct'!"

I had no intention of depriving my family of precious time, but I was certainly willing to give the contest a good try. Shortly after the contest was in full swing, one of the agents couldn't handle all the business that was coming his way.

"Would you like a client, Donna?" he asked. "We'll go 50/50." Tom was the type of guy you'd want for your brother. Pleasant, sincere and a buddy to everyone.

"Sure I do, I've hardly racked up any points towards the Bahamas."

"That trip's mine, Donna, stay back, everyone stay back, Uncle Tom's already packed."

He was well on his way to the top, far above everyone else in points and it didn't look as if anyone could dream of catching him. I took his client out the next day and was typing an offer by nightfall. "We'll split their backup listing too, okay? You're too busy to service it properly, Tom."

"I can't believe it. I've been working those folks for months and you close them in one day. How'd you do it?"

"I don't know. Got any more like them?"

"You bet I do — here." He handed me a slip of paper with a new name.

The very next day I sold the new couple a property, out of town, close to where I lived. Again we had a backup listing to share. Only problem with both deals was that both couples wanted the properties they saw so much, that they had placed 'firm' offers on the homes, against my advice. I was now pressured to sell the ones that they lived in, otherwise they would each own two properties. I'd have to sit on 'open houses' every weekend until they sold.

The first weekend approached and I decided the town home was top priority since the other clients were paying cash for their purchase and would not be as financially strapped if theirs took a while to sell.

My clients, Bob and Debbie, on the other hand, needed the downpayment from the sale of their townhouse to close their deal without any complications.

I realized I needed divine intervention. I couldn't wait for Debbie to leave. She had planned to go golfing and finally, after two hours into the open house, left. She was not the type of person that you would take out a Bible in front of and start praying.

The moment she left, I took my Bible from my purse, placed it on top of the newspaper I was reading and prayed, "Dear Lord, You know the situation I have here. This townhouse HAS to sell this weekend so that next weekend I can sit on the other property. I am not praying for greedy motives, but, I would also like the summer off to spend with the boys and it's almost June. There's a buyer out there, somewhere. Find him. Get him. Zap him here. Thank you, Lord."

I put my Bible back in my purse and resumed reading my paper. Not five minutes passed, when the door opened and someone yelled, "Yoo-hoo?"

That was it! They were here. These were my 'heaven sent' buyers. My heart pounded in my chest as if this was my very first deal. Boy, Lord, do you move fast!

"Come on in!" I yelled back nonchalantly.

"Hold it! H-O-L-D IT! We're not here to buy a house. I don't even know why we stopped, we were on our way to go grocery shopping."

"That's okay. I've got a full pot of coffee you can help me drink."

"We don't live too far from here. Got a big house with an in-ground pool. Don't know why we stopped to look at a townhouse."

I knew. I knew they were the buyers the Lord literally zapped off the street.

His wife was looking around the living room, "Awfully small, isn't it?"

"Anything would look small when you live in a big detached home." I replied, still struggling to keep from showing any anxiety. Inside I was doing a jig.

"How much did you say they want for it?" the fellow asked.

"$56,600.00. They have to sell, they've already bought another place."

"Tell you what," he continued, "I'll give you $50,000 for it."

"What are you doing, Doug? Are you crazy? What are we going to do with a townhouse?"

He hadn't even seen the upstairs! "I don't know. For fifty thousand I think it would be a good investment."

"Well, why don't you put that on paper and I'll see what I can do. Would you be willing to come to my office now and put in an offer?"

He agreed, "Sure!"

"Go up Erin Mills Parkway and I'll catch up and honk; you can follow me there. It'll be easier than trying to explain where it is." I almost broke both legs running up and down the stairs turning off lights, emptying ashtrays, clearing away coffee mugs and collecting my belongings.

I ran outside to find I had locked myself out of my car and their car was already half a block away. I ran after it.

"STOP! STOP! WAIT!"

I didn't even know their names, except that he was Doug, nor where they lived. I could just see myself putting an ad in the paper: LOST: ONE BUYER. URGENT! PLEASE COME BACK.

They spotted me in their rear view mirror and stopped. I was yelling at the neighbours, "I SOLD THIS HOUSE, SOMEONE GET A CLOTHES HANGER BEFORE THEY CHANGE THEIR MINDS!"

"Hey, didn't I go to school with you? Grade eight, right?"

"Never mind, don't ask questions, just get me in my car before those people change their minds."

The secretary had already left for the day and I had to type the offer myself.

"Why are we doing this, Doug?"

"I don't know, Doe. Beat's ME!"

"You aren't going to change your minds are you? You know once you sign this document you are committed. You're not going to stop payment on this cheque are you?" I asked peering over the typewriter. God, don't let that happen, okay?

"Oh, no. Don't worry. Once I make up my mind, that's it. I just don't know WHY I'm doing this. Instead of going to buy groceries, I buy a house. It's not like me at all-- not at all."

I ran back and forth all evening, trying to get either the vendors down in price or the buyers up. Finally after one a.m., we reached a deal. Doug was adamant about getting the townhouse for fifty thousand, and when on the third signback, he offered the ludicrous sum of $50,271.00, everyone realized he was not about to budge on another try.

"Stay and have coffee before you go home. This is a celebration."

They were such a fun couple, and in such a giddy mood, that I sat down and made myself comfortable. Once too often, he wondered out loud, wondering what ever possessed him to buy that house.

"Listen folks, I'm going to tell you why you bought that house. For all it's worth, and you can take it or leave it, but — five minutes before you came in, I had my Bible out and was praying for a buyer."

"You carry a BIBLE WITH YOU?" He blurted, spurting out coffee at the same time.

"Oh, yeah," I reached down in my purse and produced the proof. "I have one in my car, too. I was praying for a buyer and there you were."

"You mean to tell me you go to church on Sundays, too?" he asked, half in disbelief, suspecting I was kidding.

"Twice, every Sunday."

"TWICE? ha, ha, ha. WHY?"

"I don't want to miss anything!"

"Ha, ha, ha, ha, what's there to miss?"

"You wouldn't believe what goes on at our church."

"What?" He placed both elbows on the table, eyebrow raised, and leaned over very close, as if expecting me to whisper the answer. Dorothy, or Doe, as he called her, was crippled with rheumatoid arthritis and in constant pain. Her fingers were almost pointing in the opposite direction. She'd been on disability pension for three years.

"Miracles take place. We don't believe you have to accept sickness or disease. We believe the Lord CAN and WILL heal us."

"Are you putting me on?"

"Not at all. Why don't you come and find out for yourself?"

I spent about another hour telling them they could have a personal relationship with Jesus Christ and told them of the healings that I knew about personally. They agreed that they would come to church, not that morning, as it was now past three a.m. but certainly the following Sunday morning. Not that he took any of this too seriously and giggled the whole time I talked, but he was definitely coming to see what I was talking about.

Dozens of people had promised me they'd come to church and dozens never showed up, but somehow I had a feeling that they would actually show up. I felt that the Lord had more in mind for them than to just dump a townhouse on them.

I now thought I had God all figured out, down pat, and planned to pray 'in' my next buyers the same way, the following Saturday. The Lord knew that I would be up to the same tactics. Surely, I thought, if it worked once, it would work again. The other clients needed their home sold just as badly.

I soon found that the Lord was more imaginative than I could ever suspect. I woke to a dull, grey, rainy Saturday morning and called my clients asking if they'd mind if I cancelled the open house. Not only because of the rain, but I was thoroughly wiped out. Since Doug and Doe were coming to church the next morning, I couldn't catch up on my sleep and sleep in on Sunday either.

Three days later, Tom advised that an offer had come in, and he himself went out and presented the offer. The second home was sold and I could now start my summer vacation a few weeks earlier than planned.

Not only was God creative, but considerate. He didn't want me to waste an entire Saturday, stewing and in a tizzy, wondering why He wasn't sending any more buyers, when He knew all along someone was buying the home the following Tuesday, anyway.

Sunday morning, I was standing out in the hall, even ten minutes after the service started, thoroughly disappointed that I had been wrong about Doug and Doe. They never showed up. Darko insisted that I call them and urge them to come to the evening service.

"You can't drag people to church, Darko. If they don't want to come, you can't force them."

He persisted until I finally agreed to call them.

"Doug, you broke your promise. What happened?"

"You see, it's like this. . . We went to a party last night...and we told them. . . that we ran into a real estate agent...who runs around with a Bible praying for clients. . . bought a house from her. . . and now we're going to go to her church ha, ha, ha, ha. You should have heard them laugh. Anyway, we came home after four this morning and we just couldn't get out of bed, miracles or no miracles."

"Will you come tonight?"

"Can't. We're having company over for a barbecue."

"If they don't show up, will you come?" I already had a plan.

"They'll be here any minute. They'll be over here by three."

"If they don't show up, Doug, will you come?"

"You've got yourself a deal, but don't hold your breath, darling."

I quickly dialed Robin. "Robin, I don't have time to explain, but we have to pray and keep someone from going to a barbecue." It was nothing new for many of us to be praying over the phone, with each other, not knowing what exactly we were praying about. We knew "That if two of you shall agree on earth as touching anything that they shall ask, it shall be done for them of my Father which is in heaven. For where two or three are gathered together in my name, there am I in the midst of them." (Matthew 18: 19, 20).

I was sitting near the back of the church when I felt a tap on my shoulder. Turning I saw Doug shaking his finger at me, "You had that Bible out again, didn't you? They never even phoned to say they weren't coming. We waited till the last minute and they never showed up."

"Lord," I thought, 'I don't like to push your hand like this, but could you touch them tonight? We know they're not going to come a second time. It's now or never!"

Many might think that my prayers don't sound very holy or very reverent, but this is how I talk, this is how I think, this is how I am, and I don't put on any airs for God. This is how I live. I pray on the run. I pray spontaneously and He hasn't objected yet. When I have the time, I spend half an hour talking with God and get into deep and spiritual worship, but I don't live a slow, easy pace and therefore my prayer life speeds up with my feet, and I don't stop to correct or upgrade my grammar.

We never have two church services exactly the same and you never know what to expect, each Sunday experiencing a fresh new reunion with the Almighty. Tonight there would be no choir, the pastors wouldn't be preaching, there would not be a skit or a film. A lady from a Scarborough church was going to sing and minister for the entire hour and a half.

A petite blond, with a dynamic voice, took the mike and sang a love song to Jesus and then went on to introduce herself.

"I'll sing one more song and then tell you how I became saved."

It was apparent why she was going to minister and sing through the entire service; her voice was in the category of Anne Murray. You could listen to her for days, a true songbird.

"I'd like to introduce my family to you. . . Where are you? Stand up, please.. . . There they are. . . my two lovely girls and the big guy's my better half. A few years ago my youngest daughter was diagnosed as having rheumatoid arthritis."

Goosebumps crawled up and down my arm. My reaction had nothing to do with a spiritual encounter with God. Anyone, whether they believed in God, or not, would realize the significance of that statement and would break out in goosebumps, if not hives.

"My baby wasn't even five years old and her future was destroyed. I shook my fists at heaven and screamed, 'If you're up there — why did you do this?'"

Then she sang another song which relayed how God reaches down to hurting man and wipes away all his tears.

Sitting frozen, not moving an inch or a muscle, and my head pointing straight, I glanced to see if there was any reaction from Doug or Doe.

Doug's head was cocked to one side and his mouth hung open. Dorothy had tears streaming down her face and was clenching and unclenching her fists, expanding her crooked fingers.

"Praise you, Lord. Almighty Father. Precious Redeemer.

All glory and honor to Your name." I prayed. "Thank you,

Jesus. Almighty and Omniscient Saviour, we bow before You.

To the King of kings and Lord of lords, be glory forever and ever.

When you do something, Lord, you sure do it GRAND!"

After more than two years, God still overwhelms me, beyond belief, over and over. Each time I realize that He is mightier than my mind can comprehend. Majestic and Sovereign and Omnipotent. Realizing He had planned it all weeks ago: the clients; the sale; the open house; Doug and Doe driving by my sign; this service; ALL prearranged. All I had to do was go through the motions. Be obedient to His will. What would have happened if I hadn't witnessed to them? I never even attempted with the vendors, they never even knew I was a Christian. I could have missed that ever so small voice which urged, "Tell them. Tell them!"

"As everyone can see; there is nothing wrong with my precious darling. Not a trace of rheumatoid arthritis," she continued.

"I didn't listen to the rest of the message. My mind was trying to absorb and understand this new magnitude of God that He was showing me. If I turned myself to Him more fervently, listened to his voice, and obeyed His will, the earth could be turned inside out, mountains moved, and the heights of heaven reached.

The service over, I couldn't wait to hear what was on their minds. "There's a Burger King up the street. . . want to go for a coffee?", I asked hoping they wouldn't just leave without finding out down to the last detail if they had been touched.

"Wait till you hear what happened to me here, Donna. Hurry, quick, we'll follow you."

Not only had they realized that the Lord reached down to them, Doug saw a vision and most importantly was convinced Doe would be healed.

We sat there 'til midnight. Doug asking question after question.

"How? Why? How come? Where has He been till now? How can you get to be my age and not even hear of a 'born again' Christian? I went to church for years as a young guy and never met God."

"Possibly you went to a dead church that was preoccupied with dogma rather than the Living God. If you sit back and ponder over your life, there probably were many times that God reached out to you, but you weren't interested, nor were you ever told that He was there, waiting for you to submit your life to Him."

Every Sunday from there on in, rain or shine, Doug and Dorothy were at both services.

"Why do you go to church twice on Sunday, Doug?" I joshed.

"Don't want to miss anything." he'd respond in a phony, high-pitched voice, imitating my tone.

They even joined adult Sunday school. I had enough trouble getting up for the morning service, much less going an hour earlier for Sunday school.

I introduced them to Sue, and we would usually meet after the evening service for a coffee and yak for hours. At one such coffee klatch, not even two months later, Doug commented, "What I wouldn't give for Dorothy to be healed."

Sue responded, "Yes, let's pray right now for Dorothy's complete healing."

Sue led the prayer. She then took Doe's hands and moved them in a clockwise motion. We could hear bones cracking and snapping.

"I can move my wrists! Look everyone, my wrists are moving!"

We encouraged her to spend the rest of the week claiming the healing. By the following week, she could hold a mug of coffee and do her own ironing. The doctor had said her arthritis was in complete remission. She was healed, except for one finger that bent downward and was still very swollen.

"The Lord told me my finger would be healed when I got baptized in water. When's the next baptism scheduled?"

I decided, rather than constantly ask and yap at God, I would listen instead. But I was not prepared for what I heard one morning, sitting on a bench, in the hall of the courthouse, in the midst of about 600 to 700 people. A tiny lady was approaching, to sit in the only vacant spot, beside me.

The Lord spoke three words: "Witness to her."

"Lord you can't do this to me. I can't turn to a perfect stranger and ask, 'have you accepted Jesus Christ as your Lord and Saviour?' DON'T BE RIDICULOUS! I'd lose my job if anyone got wind of this. I can't; not here."

I was arguing adamantly deep in my spirit, when this little lady blurted, "Oh I just PRAY my son gets out on bail!", while turning toward me.

Say no more! Motormouth had an opening and it would be hard to stop me now. "Just keep praying, He's listening."

"Pardon?" she replied, not expecting a response because she was only using an everyday expression.

That was at nine o'clock in the morning. By one o'clock, and I had been talking continuously. She was holding on to my arm, following me to the nearby restaurant for lunch. I told her she could keep the little Bible I carried in my purse. She held it to her breast, tears streaking down her cheeks.

"For me? Oh, thank you, thank you kindly." Her grilled cheese sandwich was soggy with tears. I continued encouraging her until we had to part at three o'clock. I told her to come to church, to get her son involved in our dynamic youth group. We had a hundred or so clean cut, 'turned on to Jesus' teenagers. I told her to pray for him, without ceasing. She was reluctant to let me go.

She never did come to church, but a few months later ran up to me in the same hall, "Donna, Donna, remember me? This is my son! Praise God, he's off drugs. He got out on bail and was sent to a youth rehabilitation centre. He's cleaned up his appearance. I'm so thankful to the Lord. We even watch those Christian programs together. He says he wants to change."

I was a little ruffled to hear that she wanted to bring him to our youth group but the social worker discouraged her saying it was too religiously orientated and might be too much for him to swallow. TOO MUCH TO SWALLOW? A seventeen year old kid, out of school, out of work, on drugs and in trouble with the law, and church might be TOO MUCH FOR HIM TO SWALLOW! Maybe meeting 100 kids that didn't smoke, drink or take drugs might be a bit of a shock, but how in the world could it hurt, especially with someone who has already tried everything else. Suicide might have been his next choice.

"Just keep reading that Bible and don't you stop praying for him. Everything's going to be okay."

I thanked God daily for my boys. How proud I was of them. How far they were from the shallowness and moral decay of this world. When Dan was in grade seven, the class was given an assignment on astrology. The kids were asked to find their sign, read their charts for the following two weeks, learn the outcome and compare similarities with kids born under the same sign.

My son approached his teacher and stated he could not and would not do the thesis.

"This contradicts my beliefs and goes against the Bible." The teacher replied he already suspected as much and allowed him to do whatever topic he desired. Dan was already being called Pastor by most of the school, and many of the students sought advice from him regarding their adolescent problems. He decided to do a project on Christianity. The vice-principal felt as Dan did and commended him for not compromising his beliefs.

The following year, the principal approached me the night Dan and Mike graduated, exhorting, "You have boys you can really be proud of. You don't see many kids like them now-a-days. They're good, decent, Christian kids."

I sent her a dozen red roses the next day for those kind words.

Getting back to real estate, the contest had to be extended. Only Tom had won enough points and our other seven offices didn't even have one entrant for the big prize. It was extended six weeks, giving at least one agent from each office a trip to the Bahamas.

Technically, Tom was the only entrant and therefore an automatic winner at our office, had there not been an extension. By the new deadline, twelve more agents qualified, including myself. Everyone was to meet at our downtown location, then each group of agents, from their respective offices, entered a room, placed their calling cards into a hat, and the agent whose card was drawn was the lucky winner.

For every hundred points, you could submit one calling card. Tom, had the most, throwing in four.

I started to pray, "Lord, Tom deserves this trip, it was once his already. Stretch forth your mighty hand and intervene and block anyone else from winning. It's only fair that HE go."

"And the lucky winner i-i-s-s-s. . . Donna Martonfi. Congratulations, Donna."

"Oh, no — but — but — not me — don't give the ticket to me."

"Let's get a picture of the group of winners," they called out.

How could I win? Lord, WHAT HAPPENED?

"Tom, I'm sorry, Truly, I'm sorry."

"Don't be silly, Donna. My beef's with the company," he said hugging me. "Of all the people in the whole world, if anyone was to get my ticket, I'm glad it's you. I'm happy for you, really I am."

"I really feel bad about this, Tom."

Ben was now arguing with me, "Donna, you worked hard too. Tom had four cards in that hat and more chance than anyone of winning. He had the advantage. Stop worrying."

I grabbed each of them under the arm and we romped down Yonge Street to the car singing, "For she's a jolly good fellow, for she's a jolly good fellow." Tom whooped it up making me feel certain that there were no hard feelings. Finally, it sunk in, I WON! I'm going to the Bahamas!

But Lord, we'll have to buy Darko's ticket and we'll have to have spending money, meaning I was in possession of a prize which was going to cost me $1,500. Besides, I just came back from Barbados four months ago. Why did I win? Why? Why not Tom?

Ben had sold our other house, which had been a thorn in our side for so many years. We had received $12,500 from the city, $12,500 from our company's mortgage and $91,000 from the sale of the house, reducing our financial burden by $116,000 in less than two years. Still, I did not have money to blow and could not see the purpose for this windfall. It's not as if I needed a vacation.

I mentioned what had happened to Susan (Verna's daughter).

"This could be a test, Donna. Maybe the Lord wants you to give the ticket to Tom. Have you ever thought of that? Just how hard were you praying for him to win, hard enough to hand him the ticket?"

"I can't do that. We'd start tongues wagging all over town. It doesn't take much to get real estate agents gossiping from coast to coast. Even Darko would get suspicious if I handed some guy our ticket; Darko doesn't think the way I do. It would cause trouble all around."

"Then, Bon Voyage!"

The other Sue had a different attitude. "The Lord blessed you for being unselfish, because you weren't praying for yourself but someone else. I just know He has something very special in store for you down there. I don't know what it is; but watch real, real hard. It's going to be something magnificent."

"All I can do is wait and see if you're right."

It's amazing how the Lord used Sue and I to minister to each other. When one was down, the other was up and talking some sense into the other. We would often laugh, "It would be horrific if one day we both woke up with the glumps, THEN WHAT? Can you imagine both of us weepy or depressed on the same day? We'd keep every angel in heaven scurrying for days trying to sort out the mess."

Just to emphasize how the Lord used this unique relationship, — I was muddling over a problem for a week and it was getting progressively worse. The Lord was not answering and I got the "I feel sorry for myself" blues and at two a.m. one night was howling into my pillow, wondering why the Lord had "disconnected my line", when the phone rang.

"Donna, I don't know what this is about and I hope I didn't wake you but the Lord said He wasn't going to let me get any sleep unless I phoned you and told you to read Philippians, 4:4. Does that make any sense?"

I sat up, wiping tears away, "YES! YES! Hallelujah! Let me just get my Bible."

God had been speaking for days, but I just wasn't listening, AGAIN. Three times that week that verse was directed to my attention. I even translated that entire chapter for my mother, and STILL I missed the message. Sometimes God has to hit me over the head with a sledge hammer and He knew that I would now finally get the message.

"He said for you to read the whole thing."

Once again tears were streaming down my face, only this time I was crying for joy. I was getting the message, loud and clear.

When I finally reached Fiona to tell her my good news, that I had won the trip, she asked me to come over because she had four or five Christian girls coming for coffee. An hour after I arrived, I realized something very unusual. I had never been in a room with one Christian, much less five, where the Lord was not mentioned once.

Quickly I brought the topic around to Christ.

"You have to tell them your testimony, Donna," Fiona urged.

"I don't know where to start. Really." I had nothing to say, unusual as this may sound to anyone who knew me.

"It would take this girl all day to tell you what's happened to her in just the last couple of years and she says she doesn't know what to say." Fiona related one of the many of my so "unbelievable, it's believable" tales.

"Just listen to this; one day she was sitting beside me in church and leaned over and said, 'the Lord told me you're going to have a baby in nine months.' I responded, 'I know, for some reason I know that too.' John and I have been trying to have a baby for three years, so Steven could grow up close to a brother or sister, and then out of the blue He let us both know that this is the time. The following week He told her it would be a girl. We'll have to wait another four months to find out, won't we? You're the only one so far that's said this," pointing to her stomach, "is going to be a girl. You're outnumbered 20-1."

"If the Lord said it's going to be a girl, I'll gladly take His odds." I quipped.

"Are you girls religious?" the tiny, dark haired girl sitting beside me asked.

"HASN'T ANYONE TOLD HER?" I almost shouted. No wonder I didn't have anything to say before, I thought everyone in the room was saved. Now I had PLENTY to say. Half an hour after I started sharing with her, she unexpectedly started sobbing.

"What is it? What's wrong?"

"I've done something awful. Just last week. I can't live with it. I'm going to get excommunicated from the church if anyone finds out, even burn in hell."

Amazing how anyone could be programmed into worrying that being excommunicated from the church outweighed burning in hell.

"No. No. No, you won't. No matter what it is, Jesus Christ will forgive you. He LOVES you. He died for you. He doesn't want you in hell."

She admitted what it was that was haunting her.

"Wanda, last week you didn't know better. Accept Jesus into your heart and ask Him to forgive you and He will. Not only will He forgive you but He'll blot out that sin from your past and give you a fresh new page, never to dredge it up again."

We said a prayer and I continued, "You're a King's kid now and the only place you're going is straight up, Wanda, and don't you let anyone tell you different. You have been 'justified' Wanda. That means; just as if you never sinned. Read Galatians 2 starting at verse 16:

'Knowing that a man is not justified by the works of the law, but by the faith of Jesus Christ, even we have believed in Jesus Christ, that we might be justified by the faith of Christ, and not by the works of the law; for by the works of the law shall no flesh be justified'."

I handed her the Bible from my purse. "Read it daily, Wanda."

"For me? I couldn't keep THAT. It's too expensive."

I had been buying five dollar Bibles because I was giving away about three a week by this point, and just a few days earlier, when I had stopped to replenish my stock and Darko had insisted I buy an especially lovely, red one, that came in its own jacket.

"I can't afford to give away twelve dollar Bibles; not at the rate I've been going through them," I told him.

"Keep this one for yourself then, it's reduced from $29.95."

Since I only had fifteen dollars with me, I couldn't buy an extra one to give out.

"I have a feeling Wanda, this Bible was especially chosen for you, just a couple of days ago. I'm honored to be able to give it to you."

"No one's ever given me anything like this before. Thank you, thank you."

She ran off saying she had to start reading it immediately.

"I'm so ashamed," confessed one of the other girls, "here she's had this deep dark secret and we've been having coffee with her for months and never once shared the Lord with her. This could all have been avoided if we even said something, even just last week."

"The Lord has His timing. She was not meant to know last week, I guess. It could have posed insurmountable problems that she would not have been able to cope with then. If it happens again, at least she will have grown enough in the Lord to be more stable in trusting the Lord to solve it for her."

Wanda's life changed dramatically that day. Prior to accepting the Lord, her husband would drink, not go to work, constantly run off on her, leaving her to cope with three babies under the age of four and a half. Her life had been a disaster. Many times she had barely enough money to feed them. Her second youngest was mentally handicapped and was smaller in size, with less mental ability than her eighteen month old. He was always sickly and in and out of hospitals.

While I was vacuuming one day, the Lord told me he'd be healed. I shut the vacuum off just in time to hear a word of knowledge on a Christian program confirming that a small child was receiving a miracle.

I ran to the phone to tell Wanda. From that day on, that little boy progressed in leaps and bounds, and started talking and doing things more in proportion to his age bracket.

My mother had met Sue, Lorrie, Fiona, Doug and Dorothy, Wanda and her son, all now telling similar miraculous stories of what the Lord has done in their lives, just as He did in mine.

"I just can't believe God talks to these people and does these things for them. I just can't believe it, that's all."

"Then who does mother? Just who out there is curing all these ailments, phobias, problems and changing the lives of these people? Tell me. Surely you must realize after all you've seen and heard that someone is."

"I don't know. I've been praying to God and fasting to Saint Anthony all my life and I've never heard anyone talk back."

"That's your problem. You are making Anthony a god and the Lord says He's a jealous God. Why should He talk to you when you're busy praying to other gods."

"How can you say such a thing? He's just a saint, that's all, I'm not making him a god."

"Yes, you are. You along with millions of other people are praying all at the same time to the same saint, and therefore you consider him omniscient and omnipotent, elevating him to the level of God. A mere man could not only be at all those places to hear all those prayers, much less answer them. Only the Almighty can do that. Do you see? If Anthony could talk to you he'd be telling you NOT to pray to him but to God alone. He didn't die for your sins, Jesus did. Why, Anthony's hair must be turning white when he's told what people are doing down here regarding him."

"I never realized. I just thought I was praying EXTRA, that's all."

"When you can reach the Almighty Creator of heaven and earth, what 'extra' is there? You think Anthony or Jesus' mother knows better than God what's good for you, and when He refuses to give you something, you try to change His mind, going through Mary and the Saints? Don't you see how ludicrous it all is? See what's happened in the lives of all these people? Everyone has had a horror story of their own to tell. They've been healed of arthritis, cancer, epilepsy. They are now leading happy, changed, victorious lives. Many of them had prayed for years to 'saint this' and 'saint that'. Why is it that God answers only when they have turned from all that? There is a difference between knowing there is a God and submitting your life to Him and acknowledging what He did for you, almost two thousand years ago, and accepting His salvation. Satan knows there is a God!"

"Are you two at this again?" my dad cursed entering the room. "Jesus Christ was nothing but a space alien. We were put on this planet as rejects from another galaxy..."

"Dad, you have to stop reading those science fiction magazines. How can you read and believe that trash and not want to read the book that has the answers to every emotional, philosophical, moral, economical and spiritual problem and question on earth?"

"Sure, we need a religion to keep us from running around murdering each other and stealing from each other. That's all that the Bible is, just rules written by some smart man."

"Don't let anyone hear you talk like that, when it's obvious you haven't read it. It was written by many men, divinely inspired by God, over a period of thousands of years."

"Yeah, yeah, it says the world's coming to an end."

"See, you refuse to learn or hear anything. The world's not coming to an end, Dad. When we are on the brink of annihilating ourselves, that's when Jesus Christ will return to stop us from blowing up what He's created. That's what it says."

"They change the Bible every fifty years."

"Really, how do you explain, since they have found the 'Dead Sea Scrolls' in 1947, that they have found that it is 98.5% accurate to what was written thousands of years ago? The 1 1/2% that has been changed are expressions such as, 'I laughed so hard my head fell off', that would not make any sense to people from another era who had never used that phrase."

"You can interpret the Bible in thousands of different ways. Everyone says that."

I didn't know why I kept on. We had this conversation the year before, and the year before that, and the year before that. I persisted hoping that for once it would sink in.

"You can only do that if you dissect it sentence by sentence, not if you read the whole story. When it says that Jesus healed a leper in Galilee, then He healed a leper in Galilee, period. You don't presume the leper flew to heaven in a fiery chariot or that he became a monk and you don't build a statue of the leper and start praying to it. It means that Jesus healed a leper. Period. Many passages mean many things to many people at different times in their lives, but words and stories remain the same."

I really thought I was getting nowhere with him until the following day when my boys related what happened late that night, in front of their grandfather's house, after I had left.

Some teenagers were making noise on his front lawn in the middle of the night and he yelled at them to leave. When they refused to move, he went downstairs and started beating them up. My mother summoned the police. When asked by the officer why he had punched them, he said, quote: "They were yelling foul things at me. If it wasn't for four letter words, they would just not be able to speak at all. They should go to my grandchildren's church and see what teenagers are like. Teenagers that have never even heard such words and don't run around at night, spaced out on dope, bothering peaceful citizens."

For my father, THAT WAS PROGRESS!

"Dad maybe you would have been more effective and got them to our church if you hadn't beat them up first."

Chapter Twelve

GO TELL IT ON THE MOUNTAIN

Margie and I had a standing date for lunch every Thursday. We would meet at various restaurants and treat ourselves to a couple of hours of revelation and shop talk. Before the menu arrived she said, "I have a problem, Donna, a really big problem."

"What is it?"

"This person I know really needs help bad. Professional help. How would you suggest that someone get help, who doesn't realize that they need it?"

Oh, oh! I thought. My face must have gone beet red. Margie would have nothing to do with the Christian side of my life and didn't even want to hear about it. Now she thinks I've gone mad.

"That all depends on the problem and how close you are to the person." I tried to keep from showing I suspected she was referring to me.

"Oh they're very close. It's serious. It's ruined their life. It looks like it's getting worse."

What could I ever possibly have said to make her think my life was anything but ecstatic bliss?

"You would definitely have to do everything you could. A true friend would admire you for your concern, even if they didn't agree with you that anything was wrong."

"Not once they're fanatical."

That word really bothered me, any time I heard it. It's only the long form of the word 'fan'. Baseball fan, hockey fan, all meant fanatic, but the whole word was used only to describe Christians. It was acceptable to be a 'fan' and rearrange your whole life and everything on your calendar to sit in front of a boob tube for six hours on a Saturday, ignore your family, drink yourself into a stupor, then jump up and down, screaming and yelling and shaking your fists, if the opposing team scored a goal. You were a fan and completely normal, but if you spent six hours a week in church and spoke to God in a normal tone of voice, you were a fanatic and needed psychiatric help.

"Maybe a person is a fanatic in your eyes, Margie, only because their lifestyle and yours conflict."

"I should have used the word alcoholic, not fanatic. What kind of a lifestyle is it when you're drunk 75% of the time?"

"What are you talking about?" I didn't know if I should jump up and down with relief or reach over and throw my arms around her neck when I realized this conversation had nothing whatsoever to do with me.

"Well, I'll be honest. It's my boyfriend. They've just fired him for being drunk on the job and he doesn't even think he's anything more than a social drinker."

My temperature back to normal and my heart again beating in rhythm, I suggested she take him to church.

"Forget it. The only time he'll come to a church is if we get married but I doubt that will ever happen. I've never known an alcoholic and I am not prepared or in the mood to be a nursemaid to anyone."

"But God can change people and their problems overnight."

"Hold it. Hold it. Don't start that. You promised you'd never preach. Okay?"

By the time I got back to my office, I was, you might say, 'itching to preach', especially since I had spent the afternoon discussing a major calamity in someone's life, that didn't need or want God's intervention.

My opportunity soon became available. An agent came skipping into the office, all excited because she had just been to a psychic that foretold marvellous things for her future. She formed a small group of agents around her to repeat, detail by detail, the wondrous events that were to take place in her life.

"Susie, (not to be confused with Sue or Susan) don't say another word. Stop right there! Guys, excuse us but we have to leave right away to discuss something of top priority." I tugged at her arm. "Come to McDonald's for a coffee, I have to talk to you right away.'

She obediently followed, presuming I had a hot real estate transaction for her and babbled about the psychic all the way down the mall.

I got right to the point. "I'm not going to beat around the bush. Do you believe in God?" My question stunned her more than if I had asked "Is the world round?"

"Well, sure!"

"If I told you the Bible was the infallible word of God, the mind of God and an accurate account of history, past and present, what would you say?"

"Well — I've never given it much thought, but we have this 400 year old Bible at home that has been passed down through our family and we consider it 'holy' and a book to be respected. I'll have to invite you over so you can see it. It's written in the old scroll with 'these' and 'thous'. It's terribly difficult to understand. Anyway, why? Are you religious?"

"Not one bit, Susie. I'm a Christian."

We sat for hours while I explained the hazards of the occult and the alternate route. I think I scared her half to death once she realized where these people were getting their unique powers from.

"I just went for fun." She continued to name the various agents at our office who had been going for years and who had sparked her curiosity. I wasn't even aware that this office had become preoccupied with this, too.

"Exactly my point. Look at their lives. The people you have just named, are the three that are almost pathetic. One's as nutty as a fruit cake, the other is living hand to mouth and couldn't sell a house even in the boom and the third one is sick 90% of the time. That is not mere coincidence. I thought it was just a lot of hogwash too, until things started to slide downhill while they were all talking of greener pastures, all promising the same prosperous outcome. Except that near the end, all three had said I would be a widow by the time I'm thirty-six."

"How old are you?"

"Thirty-five. I'm not worried though, I've renounced my involvement with it and rebuked that negative destiny."

She went on to tell me that she had been secretly watching Jimmy Swaggart each Sunday morning, and that what I had just told her about Jesus Christ and salvation was exactly what he has been saying. She wanted to become a Christian, since, as she put it, "it doesn't look like it's hurt you any. Just don't tell Margie, Okay? She doesn't go for that stuff."

"I won't tell anyone at all. That part's up to you."

"By the way, why did you say you weren't religious?"

"I'm not. Religion is a man-made philosophy of man trying to work his way up to God. Christianity is God reaching down to man and having a personal and intimate relationship with His children, through Jesus Christ. Read Ephesians 2: verses 8 and 9:

'For by grace are ye saved through faith; and that not of yourselves; it is the gift of God: Not of works, lest any man should boast!"

"I had no idea you were — I mean, you're really a nice person and so honest and lovable, but I've never heard you talk like this before. I know whenever anyone in the office would curse, a dozen heads would peer over the partitions and say, 'Is Donna here? Don't let her hear that,' but I thought it was just some funny little quirk of yours. There is no one worse than me when it comes to four letter words, and you've never said anything to me."

I laughed. I had noticed the commotion many times, especially the older agents, jumping up to see if I'd get ruffled whenever someone cussed.

"You know the only thing I say and ONLY when the curse pertains to God is 'You're talking about the Lord that stretched out his arms and died for you'. There's never any reply, it just stops them dead in their tracks and they scratch their heads wondering, What brought that on?"

"I really appreciate you being so frank and telling me all this. Not many people would open up like that and stick their necks out. I'm really touched. Thanks."

Following that one 'coffee break', she would often approach my desk to share something she had heard on Christian TV, or read in the Bible. She was well on her way.

My lunches with Margie were always a little more than intriguing, but today, she especially looked like she was up to mischief.

"What would make you quit Joe's office?"

"Nothing. Absolutely nothing!"

"How about a subdivision?"

"Nothing — but a subdivision, I stand corrected."

"Well go pack your things and tell him quick 'cause tomorrow you and I have 23 homes to sell."

A real estate agent's dream come true. Twenty years, people wait in this business to get a subdivision and now she's telling me we start tomorrow.

"Joe, I love you like a brother. You and Ben and at least a dozen agents in this office are like family to me — but — Joe — SEE YA! BYE!"

"I'll get her for this. I'll get that Margie. She takes my most promising agent. She's been a pill since the day I laid eyes on her. Why me? Why does she do it to me?" he stormed.

"Keep it up, Joe. My head will swell so large I won't be able to get out through the door. You know I'll be back. I always come back. Oh, by the way, do I still get to go to the Bahamas even if I don't work here?"

"Of course you get to go. I'll kill that girl for taking you away. I'll beat her to death with your ticket. Go to your sub, Donna, get it out of your system, it's not all you think it is. You'll starve. You'll see. I hope you don't, but the market's slow and you belong here. Your desk will be waiting anytime you decide to come back."

Margie and I agreed to split the six days at the sub in this fashion. She would work, Saturdays, Sundays and Mondays, and I would work Tuesdays, Wednesdays and Thursdays. A nice gesture on her part, knowing I wanted Sunday off.

It was going to be a piece of cake! Clients coming to us instead of us chasing clients. An opportunity of a lifetime. Eight hours a day, three days a week, to do the things I did not have time for at home. I read a book a day, I crocheted a seven foot bedspread and I would even take my household bills and bookwork to do there. I was afraid one day, I'd get to the point where a customer would walk into the model home and find me ironing.

I soon became preoccupied with reading. I never dreamed Christian books could be so humorous and entertaining, as well as educational. I read many autobiographies, such as Dr. R. Eby's book, 'Caught Up Into Paradise'. It's his account of how he died and spent more than half an hour in heaven. Betty Malz had a similar experience in her book, 'My Glimpse of Eternity'. I would run out and buy ten more copies and distribute them to people I knew would benefit and be interested in the contents.

'Sexual Maturity for Women' was so hilariously funny, yet hit the nail on the head on so many topics ranging from taking everything including your kitchen sink with you on his camping trip to blubbering over soap operas through sixteen boxes of Kleenex, to the "I've got a headache syndrome', that I bought 25 copies and decided to give them out as Christmas presents.

'The Happiest People on Earth', by Demos Shakarian, hit very close to home. 'More Than a Carpenter', by Josh McDowell, was the one book I thought every agnostic and athiest should read; it would surely make them sit back and seriously question their beliefs — or rather 'lack of belief'.

I bought a copy of Joyce Landorff's, 'Tough and Tender' just before my trip to the Bahamas and planned to read it on the plane. That book in itself was the one 'opening factor' to a conversation that changed the life of yet another stranger.

I was seated in the aisle seat, when a size five (I'm a twelve), blonde (I'm a brunette), about 22 years old (I'm almost old enough to be her mother), indicated the window seat was hers. Darko had been married to me long enough to know that unless he wanted me to ruin his vacation, he'd better offer to switch seats with me, but PRONTO. We did it very cleverly. We both stood up to let her in and then I went forward first, now in the middle' seat position. A much better arrangement, as far as I was concerned. By the fifth page of Landorif's book, I was giggling noticeably.

"A comedy?" She initiated the conversation.

"No, a Christian book. It's hilarious."

"What can be even remotely funny in a Christian book?"

"I can see you haven't read any." I stopped right there knowing I had aroused her curiosity.

"Are you a Christian?"

"Uhhuummm."

"You don't look like a Christian."

"I've got my long robe and sandals in my suitcase. I'm traveling incognito."

She laughed so hard she spilled her wine all over the front of her white suit.

"OH NO! I saved for months to buy this outfit!"

"That's why I wear the dress I'm the most fed up with on planes, the one I wouldn't cry over if someone burnt a cigarette hole in."

"Why didn't I think of that? By the way, that's a lovely dress anyway. You look nice. Who'd suspect it's your reject. I should have done that."

She wasn't silent for more than half a minute, and this had been the longest I'd ever kept quiet in years. I sensed that she had to talk. She ordered another glass of wine asking, "I hope you don't mind if I drink."

"No, no. Feel free."

"You're sure, now? I'm going to have fun, really live it up."

"Good."

"Yeah, I've been saving for a long time and I'm really going to let my hair down."

"Uhhuumm."

"You don't approve of that do you?"

"What? Listen, it's your vacation."

She ordered her third glass.

"I don't always drink like this, but I want to have fun. Right?"

"I guess. Are you having fun?"

She was bouncing in her seat. "Yeah. . . this is living."

I resumed reading without making a comment. Not like me at all. I could have been at least a little bit sarcastic and said something like, "You could have fooled me". Someone knew when to button my lip.

"I'm really a 'NICE' girl, you know."

"I'm sure you are."

"I'm not loose or anything."

"Listen, please. . . why are you apologizing to me? Am I making you uncomfortable?" I couldn't figure out why I would. I had long red nails, hair down to my waist, wear lots of makeup and look as 'with it' as anyone else, but I felt like running to the john and taking another look in the mirror.

Next thing I know, she's got her head on my shoulder and she's bawling like a baby. She doesn't wear waterproof mascara EITHER and here I was worried about being drenched by wine.

"I'm so miserable. I'm so lonely. My live-in boyfriend and I don't get along. I really took the trip to straighten out my head."

I was more than aware that this seating arrangement was God's idea. There was not one other person on that plane that should have been sitting next to me or needed to hear desperately that familiar story.

"I can see into the future. It looks okay, but I've been waiting for so long, I won't be able to make it that far."

"What do you mean you see into the future?"

"I'm a witch A GOOD WITCH!" she quickly added. When she said that, I on the other hand, no longer needed this aircraft to fly. I was generating enough adrenalin to do the job myself.

"Do you believe in God?"

"Of course."

"Why are you mucking with witchcraft then? Do you know how dangerous that is?"

"It's not dangerous. I use good magic. I can even make furniture levitate. I'll show you when we get off the plane."

"God detests anything to do with magic or the occult. People who practice it are literally on the road to hell and I say that very seriously."

"Why? I've saved peoples' lives. Why would He mind if I used my powers to save someone's life?"

"What you're saying then, is that you're playing God..."

"What do you mean?"

"Since only God gives and takes life, you're elevating, and I don't mean it to be a pun, yourself to the height of God Almighty. That's exactly what Satan wanted to do; BE GOD."

"I never thought of it that way. Oh God, I only meant it for good. You see, I've had three visions of death. Twice I saw someone about to die and said nothing, and they died. The third was my sister. I saw her get hit by a green truck, so I warned her. She was extra cautious and jumped out of the way when the truck would have killed her. I saved her life."

"No, you didn't. The first two visions were real foretastes of what was about to befall your friends anyway. Whether you warned them or not. The third vision was a lie. The truck was never going to KILL your sister, the devil added that to the vision of the 'near accident' so that you could run around playing God for the rest of your life. You have to renounce your power. Look where trying to be God got Satan. Hell was prepared for him and he wants to drag you along with him."

"I have to phone my aunt as soon as we land. She has the gift too. She's the one that taught me levitation."

"Any time it surfaces, call on the name of Jesus. All the principalities in the universe have to submit to His name. You have all the power and authority of heaven and earth through His name. 'Greater is He that is in you, than he (the devil) that is in the world.'"

While waiting to pass through customs she says, "Can you help me find a nice, clean-cut guy while I'm down here?"

"I've got exactly the one," pointing out the only single agent out of our group.

"Forget it. Can't you do better than that?"

"On such short notice you want I should come up with Redford?"

"That's good. Really good. That was a Barbara Streisand imitation, right? That's really good!"

"Barbara Streisand you got, it's Redford I can't do."

The guy in front of us is chuckling, "Redford at your service."

I could write a book on that trip alone. One day, I probably will. I only want to relay some of the highlights here. Sue didn't even touch the tip of the iceberg when she said God had something special in store for me.

I have been battling the battle of the bulge since I was twelve years old. I had a thirty pound spread that would fluctuate with the weather. Twenty pounds was easy to shed, but the last ten I had only whittled off twice in my life, once so that I could fit into a size ten wedding dress and the other when I almost died with pneumonia. I was at my 'just dumped twenty' size because I knew I'd be on the beach. I started to shed two pounds a day. I ate to my heart's content, but visibly saw the fat melting. Desserts, cream puffs, anything I wanted and as much as I wanted. The pictures of the trip showed a slightly round figure melt to a SLINKY. I thought I had died and went to heaven.

Contrary to Barbados, the islanders were friendly, happy and cooperative. No one hurried. Everyone concentrated on seeing to it that you had a vacation you could write home about.

One taxi driver took us to a remote, out of the way restaurant, and then waited an hour and a half till we finished our meal to drive us back.

"Take your time" he urged, "Relax. Enjoy."

Another driver dropped us off at a 'born again' church on Sunday night and we had told him to pick us up at eight. The service didn't finish till 8:45 and we ran out apologizing.

"No need to rush. I'm cool. I wasn't going to drive off."

They didn't have their meters running either. Each time the ride didn't cost more than five dollars.

I loved the people. I commented to one chap, "If you people could just talk slower and move faster, this would be paradise."

"I can talk slower, but I sure ain't gonna move any faster."

I learn quick. I slowed down. I stopped to smell the flowers. My eyes and ears and other senses were opened to the beauty and serenity of this island, Even my vocal cords responded. Never, never, never would I allow anyone to hear me sing (except my kids of course). When we sang in church I was always ten decibels lower than anyone else. Now I was running, jogging and skipping up and down the beach singing, "Born again, just like Jesus said, born again, and all because of Calvary, I'm so glad that I've been born again." People joined in.

They stopped to learn the words, even. I didn't know if I sang on key or not and I didn't care. By the middle of the week I had half the people on the beach singing the song.

My 'Jesusitis' caught on. It was contagious. By the end of the week, I was leaving behind more than 300 friends. I had a crowd of dozens around us, wherever we went.

The first night we went to the Casino. I had gambled and played cards all my life. It was our usual pastime but I had no desire to sit at a table whatsoever. It was such an eye-opening sight I couldn't believe that I was observing. These people, although making noise and merriment, looked pathetic. They reminded me of corpses sitting around a grave yard. No life in their faces, no joy in their life. Each face as blank as the next.

A perfect place to drop innuendoes, maybe shake someone into reality that was obsessed with the momentum and speed of this environment. My Barbara Streisand voice surfaced again. Something I had never done or even been capable of before. Along with all her mannerisms and a sense of humor to match. I even stunned myself. People were visibly jolted and would turn when they heard me speak, expecting to see Streisand.

I asked if I could get a coffee. "Coffee? Sure, but you have to drink it out of a cocktail glass."

The hostess brought me a glass wrapped in a napkin so I wouldn't burn my fingers. I stood in the middle of the casino with the steamy brew. Hundreds, and I do mean hundreds of people, came up asking what I was drinking, thinking it was some new 'hot concoction.'

"It's coffee. Try it, you'll like it. Probably won't lose as much money either, drinking this stuff."

By the third night I was not the only one at the casino holding a napkin wrapped highball. There had not been ONE COFFEE VISIBLE IN THAT WHOLE PLACE TILL MINE. People only needed direction. Everyone's drinking FREE BOOZE, so they're drinking free booze.

"Do it my way and your whole trip might be a FREEBIE."

The second night we came, I made certain I was dressed to the teeth, my makeup perfect and loaded on the jewelry (within taste) to make it obvious that I could afford to be there, because people asked, "Lose your shirt? Can't play anymore?"

"Not at all. It's a lot more entertaining watching you lose your shirt — and CHEAPER TOO!", still in the Streisand voice.

Darko roamed from table to table as if he was at a fleamarket checking out the antiques, leaving me alone most of the time. I don't have to tell you that the men are on the prowl at a casino.

"Can I place a bet for you lady?"

"Sorry, I'm the bouncer, management won't allow me to pay.'

"You're really different. Drinking coffee, not playing, what are you doing here?"

"Actually I'm not the bouncer, I'm a 'Bible thumping' Christian and this is the best place on the whole island to round up converts."

After three nights, I was a known regular. Even the dealers were saying, "That's it buddy, you've had enough. Why don't you go talk to that lady and have her talk some sense into you?"

"Watch it, I'll want to start drawing wages and Streisand DOES NOT come cheap."

I had the time of my life and my audience not only enjoyed it but would get very serious.

"That's the attitude to have, lady, you're the only one in this place that's sane.

Encouraging stuff!!! I got bolder and braver. I never actually walked in with a Bible under my arm, but everyone knew where my chips were laid.

The finale, the ultimate special blessing, came when I was standing by the pool, gazing into the refreshing, inviting water, at the nine foot mark.

"Jump in," a voice inside my head urged. "Oh, oh. That's not God. I don't test God. Sorry, I'm not jumping off any tall buildings yelling, 'God save me!'"

"I taught the animals to swim. I taught you too, before you knew what fear was."

IT WAS HIM!

I dove in. When I surfaced I realized I had shortened Darko's life.

"GET OUT, GET OUT OF THERE. What are you doing? GET OUT OF THERE! GET A ROPE! SHE CAN'T SWIM!"

I wasn't swimming in the water, I was DANCING. It was almost a ballet. People had gathered. "She's a swimmer. What are you yelling about?"

I was doing a leisurely back crawl.

"She's afraid of water. She's never been in a pool past her knees. Donna, GET OUT OF THERE RIGHT NOW!"

Then he realized what I was doing was not natural. Divine intervention! He sat down and started to cry. I was laughing and crying and diving to the bottom and crying some more.

"Look, Darko — GOD'S TAUGHT ME TO SWIM!"

My arms were propped under my head and I was propelling myself back and forth by wiggling only my toes. I knew that even the best of swimmers couldn't do THAT.

"Thank you. Thank you for teaching me to swim." My only last hangup.

By the time I got out of the water, Darko was convinced I would be walking on it next.

"Don't do that to me. Why didn't you warn me? You want me to have a heart attack?"

The next night, six of us were packed into one of those long limousine taxis, including a couple we had met at the hotel and two agents from the company. They were teasing, "Well, why couldn't she walk on the water? Didn't Jesus walk on the water?"

The taxi driver threw his head back with: "You could too, mister, if you had the faith He did."

"AMEN BROTHER, AMEN!" I chorused, "YOU TELL 'EM."

What do you say when you go home after a trip like that and people ask, "Have a good time?"

"IT'S BETTER IN THE BAHAMAS" just sounds too blase.

Again our plane was the last flight in. I sat in church a few hours later, my eyes droopy, half asleep.

Someone tapped my shoulder just before the service started.

"Hi, I'm Carol. I've been trying to get hold of you. Nice tan. We're stuck for a Gal Pal. Can you come at seven p.m. on Tuesday and bring a plate of sweets and a Christmas ornament to exchange as a gift with your gal pal? Her name's Lisa."

"Fine. I'd love to."

I had Monday to get all my affairs in order and the boys settled back home. Tuesday, I was really running late and ran into a store to get an ornament. What do you get? Think quick. A white and gold angel caught my eye. Beautiful. Oooops!, were angels okay? It's funny, after three years how much you still don't know. Well, they must be okay, I figured. We don't worship them or pray to them, I'm not buying this as an object of any significance.

I ran through the cashiers.

Not until I got to my model home did I realize I would need a box, scotch tape, a card and wrapping paper. Now what do I do? I'm going straight from here and closing down early to boot.

I can't leave it till the last minute.. . . IMPROVISE!!

This 2,500 square foot home only contained one desk. PERIOD. The house was vacant and empty and if I didn't find anything in this desk I was really stuck. I rummaged through the drawers.

A large SNOOPY bag and a pair of scissors. Great, that's a start. That was going to be my wrapping paper. No scotch tape but I did have nail polish. It took some doing but I got the paper to stick to the box. It didn't look too bad, kind of cute with the large snoopy cartoon on the front. What else? Dig.

I found transferable stencils. Super. I won't need a card. I stencilled the name LISA under snoopy.

Keep digging.

Some gold, stretchy, elastic, kind of cord. I tied a bow. It took me most of the afternoon, but I ended up with a work of art. I flew over to the church only minutes before seven.

"Hey where'd you get that great Snoopy paper?"

"It was a big bag. Honest. The whole thing's held together with nail polish."

I was introduced to Lisa. Her eyes were wide with anticipation.

"I've got the nicest package here. How'd you get my name on like that?"

I was exhausted to the point where I thought my legs would just give in but I picked up momentum playing the various games and chasing the kids back and forth. We weren't sitting more than a few seconds at a time before we were back to another game, and scurrying to win some prizes.

I suddenly stopped in my tracks. There on the wall, hung a huge calendar. DECEMBER 7TH, 1982.

Now isn't that something? The Lord knew that with the trip and preparation for Christmas I would have completely overlooked that date and then hated myself for not stopping to cherish the memory of my first little darling. Here He had arranged for me to be at a party, with about twenty-five little girls, celebrating. That realization hit me hard, but not as hard as when I opened Lisa's package and found the angel she had made for me, I became too choked to speak. How appropriate. I hadn't even known at that store how that angel would reach into my heart and stir my emotions, especially since Lisa made one for me.

"Lisa, I don't think I'll soon forget this party."

My motherly instincts were stirred and I could have said a lot, lot more. I could have told her about a little girl I once had that went to be with Jesus. But this was a kid's party and not for sentimentality. I just smiled at her and I could see in her eyes that she saw the love in mine.

"Thank you Lisa, for a lovely evening."

Joyce called everyone to sit down. "We're going to end the evening by having Jane read a story. This is a secular story, girls, not from the Bible, but so beautiful that I thought it would be appropriate to read it tonight."

It was a fifteen minute story and half way through I was shaking, trying to keep from weeping. It was story about a little crippled girl who went to Bethlehem to see Jesus and she stood by his manger and started to grow big and strong and straight.

'How can it be, that Thou my Lord, should care for me? Heavenly Father, I, — I, — I don't know what to say." The sides of my cheeks were aching. I was not going to spoil this party by having twenty-five little girls and their Gal Pals wonder why tears were welling in my eyes.

Susan was sitting across the room and said, "We're going to close in prayer and I don't know why, but I sense a burden in my spirit to pray for Donna Martonfi. I don't even have my glasses on and I can't see where you are Donna, but the Lord impressed on me to pray for you tonight for some reason."

In a voice choked with emotion, I shared what the Lord was doing for me that evening. When I had finished, I was not the only one to have tears streaming down my cheeks.

All the way home, in the dark, and through healing, cleansing tears, I sang worship songs to the Omniscient One. `Why me? Why do you always do these things for me?' I went to my bedroom and took my Bible and opened it. My eyes fell on 1 Corinthians, Chapter Two:

'Dear brother, even when I first came to you I didn't use lofty words and brilliant ideas to tell you God's message. For I decided that I would speak only of Jesus Christ and His death on the cross. I came to you in weakness — timid and trembling. And my preaching was very plain, not with a lot of oratory and human wisdom, but the Holy Spirit's power was in my words, proving to those who heard them that the message was from God. I did this because I wanted your faith to stand firmly upon God, not on man's great ideas. Yet when I am among mature Christians I do speak with words of great wisdom, but not the kind that comes from here on earth, and not the kind that appeals to the great men of this world, who are doomed to fall. Our words are wise because they are from God, telling of God's wise plan to bring us into the glories of heaven. This plan was hidden in former times, though it was made for our benefit before the world began. But the great men of the world have not understood it; if they had, they never would have crucified the Lord of Glory.

'That is what is meant by the Scriptures which say that no mere man has ever seen, heard or even imagined what wonderful things God has ready for those who love the Lord. But we know about these things because God has sent His Spirit to tell us, and His Spirit searches out and shows us all of God's deepest secrets. No one can really know what anyone else is thinking, or what he is really like, except that person himself. And no one can know God's thought except God's own Spirit. And God has actually given us His Spirit (not the world's spirit) to tell us about the wonderful free gifts of grace and blessing that God has given us. In telling you about these gifts we have even used the very words given to us by the Holy Spirit, not words that we as men might choose. So we use the Holy Spirit's words to explain the Holy Spirit's facts. But the man who isn't a Christian can't understand and can't accept these thoughts from God, which the Holy Spirit teaches us. They sound foolish to him because only those who have the Holy Spirit within them can understand what the Holy Spirit means. Others just can't take it in. But the spiritual man has insight into everything, and that bothers and baffles the man of the world, who can't understand him at all. How could he? For certainly he has never been one to know the Lord's thoughts, or to discuss them with Him, or to move the hands of God by prayer. But, strange as it seems, we as Christians actually do have within us a portion of the very thoughts and mind of Christ.' (TLJB)

I was again in His presence as on that day many years ago, only now I knew 'Who it was that I have believed, and am persuaded, that He is able ...'

That evening He explained His first words to me; 'I did not do this — but I will show you how great I am!'

I often wondered what He meant, 'I did not do this — who else could? He took me back to my pregnancy, to a night when Judy and I had picked up a OUIJA board and wanted to know if I was having a girl or a boy. We pressed for an answer over and over. Fright filled my being when it answered and spelled out:

GORDANA'S BABY HAS A BAD HEARD

We could not figure out if it meant h-e-a-r-t or h-e-a-d. But we were both convinced we had reached the spirit world. She had never known or heard my real name. Only my parents called me and had christened me GORDANA; a name which was changed to Donna, by the time I was eleven.

"I did not harm your daughter, I only stood back and allowed you to suffer the consequences of your foolish actions. I allowed what you had gone searching for, to show you the magnitude of the depth of darkness you were flirting with."

Then in my mind's eye I saw Jesus standing, holding my baby girl in His arms.

The New Year ahead really stumped me. Margie and I were not making any money. I don't mean hardly any, I mean none at all.

"Lord, what's wrong? I'm putting in the hours, I'm using them constructively. Am I not supposed to get paid for work I do? I don't understand, TALK TO ME.

SILENCE.

April, Margie threw in the towel.

'Sorry Donna. This was all a mistake. Who would know the market was going to be so bad."

"Don't quit before spring. Spring is always good. You're pulling out just before the windfall."

Spring came and went. My new partner and I sold O-N-E house. To make matters worse, he had our company thrown off the sub for saying, in front of a client, while the builder was standing there yet, "I learned at the seminar not to trust builders."

"NOW WHAT LORD? WHY DID YOU BRING ME HERE?

Am I supposed to go back to Joe's office. Is that it?"

One word: "NO."

I was soon offered another subdivision and would have to start sitting on the site in July.

"I'm not giving up my summer with the kids, Darko."

"Take it. All the homes sell by September and you'll be able to take the winter off, until next spring.

I argued, "The kids go back to school in September. I don't need to be home then."

"Donna, you'll be missing out on a small fortune. You can make thirty thousand dollars by September." he added.

I still wasn't convinced, "What if they don't sell like the last bunch?"

"They will. They have to."

I reluctantly spent my summer sitting in a trailer. No water. No plumbing. To make matters worse, my new partner wanted every other weekend off. I would zoom to church every second Sunday, directly from the subdivision... dirty, dusty and grubby.

Not only did none of the homes sell by September, when the builder saw how slow the market was, he didn't even BUILD the houses.

"Lord, something's wrong. Talk to me. I've never been big on patience and now it's been nine months since I've had any income except what I've made at court. . . that's patience, right? I now have patience."

Even though He was silent, I felt deep in my spirit that there was something I was supposed to be doing. WHAT? I didn't understand. He was silent; yet still working miracles in every other aspect of my life.

Uncle Tom was advised he had cancer throughout his whole stomach and would have to have immediate surgery to have his stomach removed. We figured he wouldn't last till Christmas. He was not a believer. I asked the church, now blossomed to a large congregation of about 700, to pray on the day of his operation. When the doctors opened him up, half his stomach was raw flesh, but it was definitely not malignant.

I told him we had prayed for him after he had recovered. TODAY, he's a believer!

I witnessed with greater power and to more people than I had ever before. A waitress in the restaurant that many of us went to after Sunday morning service, came over to me and asked, "What is it about you people? You don't get upset if we spill things. You don't hurry us. You are all smiles and happy faces. We want to know what kind of 'happy pills' you're taking.

"We're hooked on Jesus. It's guaranteed to put a smile on your face."

She was now sitting down with us, "I don't care if I get fired for this but I've got to hear this. . . It's true. You should see the people that come in here, shouting and pushing their kids, growling at us. You people are phenomenal. What church do you go to?"

"Mississauga Gospel Temple." Since her job was in jeopardy, I suggested she come over to my house the next day and I'd fill her in. She came and I led her to the Lord.

Everything but real estate was running smoothly and according to God's purpose.

At times I could almost reach out and touch the answer and yet I could not grasp it.

"Lord, I'll just lean and rely on you as long as it takes. I'm willing to go anywhere and do anything, but I have to know what that is. Show me. Please."

With school starting, the hustle and bustle to prepare for my boys' first year in high school, and Steven starting at the new school for gifted children, (we had recently found he had a genius I.Q.), I planned to phone Darko at work and tell him not to call me at midnight. The company went on twelve hour shifts so that he left by eight p.m. and would generally phone around midnight when he could catch a break. Twice he called to ask why I hadn't prayed for him that night.

"I can always tell when you forget to pray. It's different. Everything goes wrong. Nothing goes right. When chaos breaks out, I know you've forgotten to say a prayer for me."

He was right both times. I would get preoccupied with someone else's need and forget.

"Honey, don't call tonight. I'm going to bed early."

"Are you okay? It's not even 9:30. What's the matter?" he sounded worried. I explained that I was just burned out and needed the extra sleep.

"OK. See you in the morning."

My head hit the pillow and I was out like a light. I thought I had only been asleep a short while when the noisy ringing of the phone disturbed me. It was daylight. I peered at the clock. Nine a.m.

RING. RING. RING.

Go away. I'm not going to answer it. If it's the court calling for a last minute bail hearing, I'll have to go in. I just can't, not today.

Ring. Ring. Ring. Ring. Ring. Ring.

The phone had rung so many times, I knew that whoever it was, knew I was there. Now more fully awake, I realized it must be Darko, otherwise he would be home already.

"Hello?"

"Mrs. Martonfi? Your husband's had an accident at work."

"You must have the wrong number, my husband's already left work. He's not there."

"Mrs. Martonfi, your husband has been hurt, do you understand what I'm saying?"

My mind continued to reject what was being said. He's no longer on machinery, doesn't work with tools, the union won't let him lift a finger. How could he get hurt?

"It can't be him. He's already left the plant." I desperately argued.

"He's at the Burlington Hospital. He's in surgery. Do you understand?"

"NO! NO!!! LORD! NO! HELP!!"

He kept talking but I couldn't even hear the words.

"I'll be right there."

The room was spinning one way and I was spinning with PANIC.

I dialled "0". "Operator, please find a number for me — connect me, please."

"I'm sorry ma'am, we cannot assist you."

"I can't see. I can't find my glasses!" I was crying into the phone.

"I'm sorry ma'am I cannot assist you, call information and write the number down big."

"P-L-E-A-S-E, I have to talk to my pastor."

She must have thought someone had died. "OH! I'll connect you, what's the name?"

HURRY! - HURRY BEFORE I FALL APART.

"Hello, M.G.T." the voice answered.

"I HAVE TO TALK TO PASTOR FRED," my voice was so frantic the youth pastor replied. "RIGHT AWAY."

The phone went dead. He disconnected me.

NO LORD, HELP! I would have to start all over again.

I got the same operator. One chance in a thousand. As soon as she heard me she had me reconnected within seconds, and without asking for the name of the church again.

"PASTOR FRED, DARKO'S BEEN HURT. I CAN'T EVEN PRAY." With those words, he started to pray and a peace and calmness engulfed me that cannot be merely explained with 'a peace that passeth all understanding'. I was completely coherent and coordinated and knew that everything would be fine.

I JUST KNEW.

"What happened?"

"I don't know, I was too upset to listen, something about his arm."

"What hospital is he in?"

"I don't know. Some name in Burlington. Why would they take him all the way to Burlington?"

"I know which hospital it is. J. Brant Memorial. Would you like me to come over and drive you there?"

I was so calm and thinking logically that I surprised even myself.

"No, thank you. I won't have my car with me to be able to get home then. Could you give me the directions?"

I wrote them down on a piece of paper.

"Call me as soon as you're able to see him and I'll come right over. And don't worry, we'll be praying. The Lord is in control."

I knew the Lord was even in control of my car. I was not driving that car. I have no sense of direction and once got lost just walking to a mailbox to post a letter. Anna lived in Burlington and although I had been to her home dozens of times, I never found it on my first try. I'd miss the signs and drive back and forth wondering if I was traveling north or south. The car knew exactly where it was going even if I didn't, and took all the right exits.

I arrived at the hospital by 10:30 and was informed Darko was still in surgery. The surgeon would see me as soon as he could. I was told his arm was almost cut off.

"When did it happen?"

"He went into surgery about five a.m."

"Five a.m." It's almost eleven. The nurses in the intensive care ward were more than considerate, running back and forth bringing me coffee after coffee from the cafeteria so that I wouldn't miss the surgeon when he came out.

I informed Pastor Fred that I still knew nothing, and that I would keep him posted. I phoned my parents asking if they would get the boys after school and take them home with them and feed them, since I would probably be there all day. Darko's parents were vacationing in Yugoslavia. I called Darko's sister and my office.

At noon I rapped on the door of intensive care again. "Sorry, he's in the recovery room and they won't allow you in there."

One of my friends had a baby just a few days before and they let her BOYFRIEND in the labour room to watch, yet they wouldn't let me in to see my husband in recovery!

"I'm sorry, that's the rules." She replied in a soft voice, sensitive to my frustration.

A few minutes later I was advised he would be brought down from recovery as soon as the staff was back from lunch at one o'clock. Each minute that ticked by was now an eternity. I started to worry for the first time since I prayed with Pastor Fred. Why won't they let me see him? Has his arm been amputated? He'll be coming down from recovery so he must be okay.

I saw a stretcher being wheeled toward my direction, I ran to meet it. My face broke out in a grin from ear to ear. He was all there. A cast, three times the size of one they put on broken arms, showed the tips of all five fingers.

"Thank you, Lord."

In the time we waited for Pastor Fred to arrive, he told me what had happened. At about two in the morning, he was crossing the conveyor when it started up and threw him off balance. He went flying, shooting his arm forward to break the fall, only he had slammed it on a jagged trunk frame, and cut it to the bone; cutting through the nerves, the tendons, everything, including both arteries. His pant leg had caught on the conveyor belt and he would have been crushed to death had a worker not seen him from the cat walk and ran and pressed the STOP button.

Holding his own wound, which was squirting blood in every direction he was driven in a plant vehicle to one of the main entrances. The buggy had so much blood on the floor that it seemed he had bled every drop he had. It took the ambulance almost 45 minutes to find him. The factory is the size of a city, with many gates and entrances. By the time they transported him to the first hospital, the doctor advised that he had been without blood and the nerves were completely severed for so long that the only alternative would be to amputate. If they could find someone to reattach everything, it would probably have to be amputated at a later date. Too much time had elapsed.

He prayed with all his might, harder than ever in his life. Finally, a young surgeon in Burlington was willing to try to save his arm and they transferred him there.

"And so here I am," he says.

"Why didn't anyone call me till 9:30? You could have died."

"I insisted they not call you till then."

"WHAT????"

"I knew you were tired and didn't want you driving around at night chasing ambulances."
"Don't you ever do that again, you hear?"

When Pastor Fred arrived, just a matter of 45 minutes or so after Darko was wheeled from recovery, he was STUPIFIED to see Darko babbling a mile a minute and me with absolutely nothing to say, just sitting there.

"Darko, I haven't heard you say this much in all the time I've known you. You look fine, too. Donna, you look awful. Darko get up. . . Donna lay down."

You would never suspect that he had just undergone five and a half hours of micro surgery. Had I seen the doctor before he began to operate I wonder if I would have allowed him near my husband. He looked like just a young kid and wore more jewellery and gold than Mr. T. I couldn't even imagine that this man was a genius in his profession, but he was!

He was very pleased to see the results a few days later. "Looks like I've done a pretty good job."

"You might be a great surgeon, and you might know how to stitch and sew and mend, but I know the HEALER himself and I'm sure He was looking over your shoulder."

"It's going to take about a year for the entire healing, if things go well," this young doctor reported. "Nerves grow back at an inch a month or a millimeter a day. Since the cut's about twelve inches from the tips of your fingers, I figure about a year. Also I don't know yet if I've hooked up the right tendons to the right fingers. We might need additional surgery. I hope everything goes okay. It's going to deteriorate before it gets better, the skin and muscle will atrophy."

The entire time Darko was in the hospital, we could FEEL THE PRAYERS of our dedicated family of God. We knew the origin of each and every prayer. They were almost a visible element you could see and reach out to touch.

His peace was constantly evident and present through this period which otherwise could have been an ordeal. His promise states: 'I will never leave you nor forsake you.' (Hebrews 13:5) WHAT A PROMISE!

TWENTY-FIVE DAYS later Darko was back at work. He progressed at a phenomenal speed, months ahead of where the doctor predicted he would be. All of the tendons connected properly and the nerves were already regenerating in most of his fingers. His employer and the compensation board admitted that some people take more than twenty-five days off when they merely stub their toe.

Shortly after he was released from the hospital, we had Pastor Fred and his family over for Sunday dinner and spent most of the afternoon discussing all the blessings the Lord had bestowed on us in the past three and a half years, most of which they had not even been aware of.

"I'm so grateful the Lord decided to let me keep him a while longer. I guess He's not in need of an electrician as badly as I am of a husband."

When Pastor Fred moved to the piano and asked for requests, I pointed out that I was not even aware that he could play. Mickie, his wife, was the Sunday organist, and I thought his only gift was preaching and singing.

"I so envy people that can sing, but people who can both play and sing, get my undivided attention and admiration."

A silent voice said, "You can type."

I laughed to myself; so can Stevie, big deal!

The following Tuesday night I was in the ladies' room when a girl asked if I was there for choir practice.

"What I would give if they would let me near a choir. As a matter of fact, I know I'm going to live a very, very long life; when the angels heard me sing they suggested I remain down here as long as possible."

She replied, "Don't be so hard on yourself, I'm certain you can do something to compensate for it."

Again that same voice, "You can TYPE."

That morning I felt led of the Lord to attend Dave's Bible class, however in less than an hour, I wondered what I was doing there. The leader, Dave, was asking what we could do to reach out to the hurting world, to coworkers and neighbours that needed a touch from the Lord. Many were replying that their coworkers didn't even know that they were Christians and they found it very difficult to share the things of the Lord with people who were not open to the subject. Some admitted that they only shared their faith with neighbours in life and death situations, and were otherwise very timid.

"What am I doing here, Lord, I'm certain that I belong in one of the other two classes where I would benefit from the teachings. I can hardly sit still and not take over this meeting with ideas about how to tune into You and then pick out people in crowded environments who need to hear the life changing message of the gospel."

"YOU CAN TYPE." Loud and clear, I heard the same three words again. On my way home I examined the meaning of those words. Type envelopes? Is that it? What would I mail out in envelopes? I passed the stage of typing envelopes for a living by the time I was seventeen. Why would I go back to typing envelopes with the qualifications I have to my credit NOW?

"YOU CAN REACH 100,000 LIVES!"

100,000 envelopes, with 100,000 WHAT inside? Cards reading; 'Jesus Loves You'? A bumper sticker would be more effective and a lot less work and eventually be seen by more than 100,000 people. 100,000 Bibles would be appropriate but there is just no way I could afford the postage, much less that many Bibles.

I'VE GOT IT !!! A BOOK !!!!!! YOU WANT ME TO WRITE A BOOK! All those hours wasted at the subdivision, I could have written one already. WHY HADN'T I THOUGHT OF THAT BEFORE — As soon as I reached home I grabbed paper and pencil and started writing. Darko was ecstatic.

"It's about time. I've been telling you to write a book for years and years. People need this, they want to know that miracles do exist and are happening every day. The media will never tell them, YOU have to. They need the assurance that God is alive and cares."

At four a.m. he sat up in bed and said, "You don't have to finish it tonight, you know."

I couldn't stop. Once I started, this story just poured out of me, although the whole time I kept telling myself this was just a silly notion, it could never get published, I would probably stop in the middle and not finish it for decades. The Lord had His reasons keeping me up that evening. He knew, like everyone else, that He could never WAKE me up at the ridiculous hour of five in the morning, He knew I would have to be kept awake and alert. The Jim Bakker program came on and was my confirmation that this project was initiated by the Lord.

"There is someone out there right now. God wants to use you to bless others for His Kingdom. Be willing to be used of God. Be obedient. God will vindicate those who stand up for HIM. Don't turn your back. God doesn't have to use you; He can use someone else. Choose to be used of God. God's calling some of you today. Listen to this song — God's speaking."

A PERSONAL MESSAGE TO ME, that's what it was. As long as I live I will never foret the words to the song that followed:

YOU BELIEVED IN ME   by Guy Heath

You believed in me
Brought me back to Calvary
Thank You eternally
You believed in me;
You believed in me
You saw what I could be
While others just shook their head
And said just let her be;
But You believed in me
You brought me back to Calvary
Thank You eternally
You believed in me;
The frustration that I felt inside
Was hard to understand
I failed to live according
To the way you'd planned
But patiently you took the time
To work on me once more
To make a clear reflection of you Lord.
You believed in me
Brought me back to Calvary
Thank you eternally
You believed in me;
Now some call me unworthy
Of the trust you placed in me
They said that I should step aside
Let others work for thee
And then You said so tenderly
That I have been restored
I'm not perfect, just forgiven by my Lord.
You believed in me
You saw what I could be
While others just shook their heads
And said just let her be.
You believed in me
Brought me back to Calvary
Thank You eternally
Thank You, Thank You, Lord.

I couldn't wait to get to the subdivision to have the eight hours of privacy I could devote to this book. Shortly after I had arrived, Marlene called to see how things were going. She was a deeply intense, lovely, spirit-filled, Christian friend. Many times over the years she had been given 'words of knowledge' by the Lord.

I told her about my book, and she suddenly said, "Donna, I received something in the mail today from a close and dear friend and for some reason have to read it to you. It's a poem she wrote. Her name is Hilda Schnell. I just know there is something in it for you."

As soon as I heard the title, I picked up my pen and flipped back to the first page I had written, and wrote 'UPHILL CLIMB' on the top of the page. I knew this would be the title of my book. It wasn't catchy and I knew those two words would not bring thousands running to buy it; I only knew that was what the Lord wanted me to call 'OUR' book.

Your life blooms with beauty
As He etches
on your spirit
Traits of His own flawless character —
How pleased He is
To watch you grow
In His grace and knowledge,
Both through the smooth times
And the rocky ones;
Each experience, in its turn,
Brings a fresh insight,
A new glimpse of His love
and great mercy and patience —
The love that places us in His lap,
With strong arms about us,
No matter how far we think we've fallen,
How irretrievable we believe we are —
He longs to hear our humble cry,
Our penitent heart's plea;
More than even this,
He yearns to restore us.
To fill our lives with His fullness
Where only emptiness has existed

And oftentimes persisted
He has set us free!
Free to be ourselves,
Only growing in Him.

'A new glimpse of His love', each and every day of my life. I'm not writing this book to draw glory or attention to myself. All the glory goes to the Lord Jesus Christ. I am no one special. I am certain that every Christian living the spirit filled life could write such a book testifying of miracles and 'God-incidences' in their lives. Intervention by God in the Christian's life is not the exception but the norm.

Do you have a mountain you've tried to climb over, crawl under, go around or through? My prayer then, is that this book has shown you the way! The 'TRUE WAY'!

'But, also, if ye shall say unto this mountain, be thou removed, and be thou cast into the sea; it shall be done and all things, whatsoever ye shall ask in prayer, believing, ye shall receive. (Matthew 21:22)

Made in the USA
Middletown, DE
17 March 2021